tangerine

D1326605

Published in 2014 by Goodman
An imprint of the Carlton Publishing Group
20 Mortimer Street
London W1T 3JW

10 9 8 7 6 5 4 3 2 1

Text © tangerine, 2014
Design © Carlton Books Ltd 2014

All rights reserved. This book is sold subject to the
condition that it may not be reproduced, stored in
a retrieval system or transmitted in any form or by
any means, electronic, mechanical, photocopying,
recording or otherwise without the publisher's prior
consent.

A CIP catalogue record for this book is available
from the British Library.

ISBN 978 1 78313 007 8

Printed in China

tangerine

25 insights into extraordinary innovation & design

Antonia Higgs

14-10-2014

Antonia Higgs

Foreword by Datuk' Professor Jimmy YK Choo OBE

GOODMAN

Foreword
Datuk' Professor Jimmy YK Choo OBE

Designing shoes that are comfortable but look beautiful is a skill that is honed and crafted; one that can be passed to future generations. Remaining true to your passion for your craft while growing a global business requires complete faith in your ability to deliver meaningful change.

In February 2013 I was invited to be a juror for the Red Dot Design Awards and it was here that I first met Martin Darbyshire, CEO of tangerine, who was a fellow juror. From humble East End beginnings, very similar to my own, tangerine have been on a 25-year journey around the world; asking questions, challenging convention and creating solutions that have changed the lives of both ordinary people and businesses. And in all that time they have remained true to their passion for design.

In this book, tangerine share insights and stories from that journey. They demonstrate the variety of challenges they have faced and their numerous approaches to finding the best answers. In doing so, they share experiences that both students and industry leaders can learn from and apply.

I wish them every success as they continue their journey.

25 years of tangerine

It was the year the Berlin Wall fell and the World Wide Web was born. It was the year Salvador Dali died and Margaret Thatcher became a grandmother. The year Arsenal won the league in the last minute of the last game of the season.

Meanwhile, in the front bedroom of a Victorian terrace in north London, just yards from where Arsenal's stars were parading their trophy, two young designers were unpacking boxes of office supplies, an original Macintosh computer and a laser printer.

It was the moment that, for them, would mark 1989 with the greatest personal significance. It was the birth of tangerine.

Twenty-five years on and the little design company that began life in an Islington spare room is now regarded as a global player in the industry, a catalyst in changing the philosophy of boardrooms around the world and a highly respected voice in considering the very future of design itself.

This book marks the 25th anniversary of tangerine, revealing key insights behind 25 extraordinary projects undertaken by the celebrated design house over the years. But it is not a history book. It is not a tale of reminiscence or nostalgia. This book takes the events of tangerine's past to consider the place of design today and, vitally, where it might go tomorrow.

In 1989, Martin Darbyshire and Clive Grinyer, two friends who had met at the Central Saint Martins College, decided to pool their talents and set up a design consultancy. Britain was in the midst of a sapping recession; the papers were filled with gloomy stories of striking dockers, tube workers and ambulance drivers.

But there was also optimism in the air – the Berlin Wall had fallen, Nelson Mandela was in talks with South Africa's President while economic and democratic reforms in the Far East all suggested the world was opening up. It was a time for ambition – and tangerine's founders had plenty of that.

When they moved from the spare bedroom of Darbyshire's home to a studio in a converted warehouse in London's East End, other young talent sought them out, wanting to join the team. Among those who followed the smell of fresh emulsion to Hoxton Street were Peter Phillips and Jonathan Ive, the man destined to become arguably the world's most influential designer at Apple.

tangerine had quickly won a reputation for fresh and exciting thinking. The young partners saw themselves as foot soldiers in a product design revolution – attempting to shift its focus from quality control and concurrent engineering to consumers and creativity. An early company brochure was based on the theme 'products for people' – a radical battle cry in an industrial landscape where disciplined management and standardisation were seen as the keys to survival.

The founding partners may have been design idealists, but they were also astute enough in business to recognise how the dramatic geo-political change sweeping the planet might present opportunities. From the very beginning, tangerine were thinking globally. And the company's current structure reflects that long-running international focus, with clients around the planet and design talent from every continent.

Alongside Darbyshire, now the CEO, are Matt Round, the Creative Director and company President Don Tae Lee. The London studio includes designers from France, Japan, South Korea, New Zealand, Norway, China and across the UK. In 2004 the company's second studio was opened in Seoul and, more recently, tangerine has set up an office in Porto Alegre in Brazil, once again showing the company's commitment to emerging markets.

This international focus has won them a reputation for helping established manufacturers regain leadership in domestic markets and expand into new ones. Their experience of bridging cultural divides and penetrating crowded trading environments is reflected, not only by the make-up of their team, but also in their range of clients: from Nikon and Toyota in Japan to Korean giants Samsung and LG; from a Brazilian shoe company to a Dutch bed manufacturer; from global brands like Huawei in China to a local hairdresser in Edinburgh.

tangerine's determination to challenge received wisdom with a commitment to successful innovation has never wavered. They were among the first to incorporate 'design thinking' into the process – indeed, the phrase was coined in their second brochure, 'the tangerine book'.

From the start they stressed the importance of seeing a product from the consumer's viewpoint, of understanding the user's needs and motivations, as well as setting a clear business context. But philosophy alone is not enough; great design cannot be learned from a book or by applying a set of rules. It requires talent, hard graft, and the wisdom that comes only from experience.

The input of consumers within the design process is important, but conventional market research can only gather opinions about past experience. Successful innovation is about unimagined possibilities, potential experiences, which focus groups and interviews will always struggle to reveal. While such techniques have a place, sometimes their inevitable emphasis on gross negatives can be misleading, drowning out insights that might lead to a design breakthrough.

tangerine's three concept machines for Apple, undertaken by Darbyshire, Grinyer and Ive in 1992, reflect the company's long-standing dedication to challenging convention, predicting the future and visualising how design can respond. The beautifully detailed concepts were the product of extraordinary design ability, imagining futuristic machines that no focus group could ever have begun to conceive.

Within Ive's 'Folio' concept, for example, were the germs of what would one day be called an iPad. Apple's then head of industrial design, Robert Brunner, still speaks of his admiration of tangerine's commitment, not just to make beautiful objects but to bring them to market.

The design and installation of the world's first fully flat Business Class bed for British Airways is a case in point. The airline's executives needed to be convinced to take the huge commercial gamble represented by tangerine's proposal. It was a challenging time for the aviation industry and

Above: Hoxton 1990, left to right, Clive Grinyer, Peter Phillips, Martin Darbyshire, Jonathan Ive.

"London at that time had a strong product design scene and here were some very talented guys in a great little studio; completely different to what you would find in the States. We wanted them as a group to help us think about this future challenge. The concepts they created were very clean, very tight, unique and they didn't just want to make a beautiful object but were committed to see it through manufacturing and make it happen."

Robert Brunner former Head of Design, Apple Inc.

Below: Bermondsey 2014, left to right, Don Tae Lee, Matt Round, Martin Darbyshire.

there were many senior executives urging caution. But the potential of the design solution was effectively communicated to the BA board members, who decided to take the risk.

The flat-bed seat won numerous awards for its beauty and ingenuity, but for tangerine the achievement went beyond design plaudits. It was about transforming a business; in this case transforming an entire market. tangerine's mission is to deliver unimagined change in products, services and experiences – doing what it takes to guide a client to where they want to get.

From its very beginning, the company has tried to help businesses see beyond the obvious, to offer fresh thinking on what really matters, joining the dots so everyone recognises what change might bring. The genesis of the success with BA, for example, was a deeper understanding of what had meaning for business travellers.

For tangerine, the last quarter of a century has been about learning, evolving and adapting to new circumstances – but without ever losing sight of the goal. Such resilience has been founded upon seven attributes:

Ask the right questions

Great design is born of humility – a recognition that even the wisest heads must still ask the right questions before they can find the right answers. tangerine's experience and expertise means they have the confidence to challenge assumptions, to keep an open mind, to stand back and re-examine the relationship between a business and its strategy, a product or service and the consumer, between design and behaviour. Such an approach keeps the design process fluid, creating tailored solutions for specific client needs.

Unlock key customer insights

Apple founder Steve Jobs famously told an interviewer, "it's really hard to design products by focus groups. A lot of times, people don't know what they want until you show it to them." It is a sentiment long accepted at tangerine, where enormous value is put on unlocking customer insights – analysing the behaviours and attitudes of potential consumers to create new products or services that they never imagined could exist.

Shape the right design strategy

Having unlocked the insights, the challenge is to incorporate that knowledge in a coherent and effective design strategy. It sounds self-evident, but achieving synergy across marketing, manufacture, design and R&D is an art. When it works, the results can be far greater than the sum of their parts – quite simply game-changing. For tangerine, the approach with the Sky+ box, perfectly combining innovative technology and brilliant design, is an example of a strategy that ultimately changed an industry.

Harness the potential of ideas

Words like creativity and innovation are often tossed about in a rather casual way, but the real skill is in turning a bright idea into transformational change – linking technological advance with unmet human desire. At tangerine, great store is put in creating the perfect conditions to imagine the future. For example, with the Blink camera, designers were deliberately freed from the constraints of the market. What emerged was a device that incorporated features years ahead of their time – early versions of the now ubiquitous LCD displays, memory cards and digital photo albums.

Find gaps a business can own

Former US Defense Secretary Donald Rumsfeld once had reporters scratching their heads when he spoke about 'unknown unknowns', intelligence you don't even realise you don't know about. For designers, it is often the 'unknown unknowns' of a product's market that are vitally important. Discover those, and you can find the gaps a business can own. tangerine's work with BA, began with designers working out the unknowns of passengers' desires and the aircraft cabin dimensions. By identifying previously unidentified potential, tangerine were able to help the business prosper.

Tell stories

The human brain is hard-wired to enjoy stories. Constructed narratives help us make sense of the complex world around us. Designers at tangerine believe that telling a story is a vital component of any successful brand and design strategy – exploiting the emotional engagement between an experience and a consumer. When they worked with South Korean cosmetics giant AMOREPACIFIC on branding for the global market, the focus was on establishing a credible narrative for the company itself. A very different commission, designing the Survival Knife for Wilkinson Sword, also required the team to identify a story for the consumer to buy into, a tale told through a simple blade and handle.

Deliver the best solution

From the very beginning, tangerine has never lost sight of the ultimate goal for any design company. That's the reason, above all, why they are still around to celebrate their 25th anniversary. The 'best solution' doesn't always mean the 'best design' or the 'best product'. It is about compromise when necessary and courage when required, ensuring that you bring a brand,

Left: 2014 tangerine, Seoul, South Korea.

Above: 2014 tangerine,
London, United Kingdom.

service or product to the highest level possible and securely to market. It is about delivering the best possible balance of creative experience and business value.

These seven guiding principles are not a checklist; a series of boxes to be ticked. They often overlap, sometimes contradicting each other. But with these seven attributes, tangerine has been able to remain a vital force in an industry that has undergone extraordinary change in the last 25 years.

And tangerine knows the industry is changing still. These days, consumers don't just want to buy a product; they want to buy into an experience. Crowded lives mean people increasingly seek simplicity and clarity rather than variety or complexity, but they also put a high value on style and meaning. They demand the very best of design.

This is the paradox to be overcome: designers must understand the multidimensional nature of 21st-century living, embrace its variation and its intricacy, but offer experiences that are sincere, authentic and resoundingly clear.

This, then, is a huge moment for designers and for businesses. Our understanding of what lies behind behavioural change is developing rapidly, just as new global markets open up. Competition is more intense and consumers are more informed than ever before. Being different or better has never been more challenging.

The good news is that design still has much more to offer; it is far from reaching its full potential. Business needs to be encouraged to take notice – to embed design in its very culture. For those who recognise those opportunities, the rewards may be great indeed. For tangerine, this is a time for optimism.

1989 was the year when the planet started to shrink, the year the possibility of a truly global market opened up as the Berlin Wall fell and the World Wide Web began, the year when design had to respond to a dramatically changing world. Twenty-five years later and tangerine is still pioneering ground-breaking design, still delivering extraordinary competitive advantage for its clients.

01

Timeless beauty is sculpted from simplicity. The gift of the great designer is to breathe life into the commonplace, releasing unimagined value.

The comb that's anything but humdrumm

Brian Drumm | 1990

Left: The Flatliner comb.

Below: Models showing
Flat-top hair cuts.

Great design can transform the practical and everyday into something beautiful and timeless. The Flatliner comb is an example of just that.

The story began with former Scottish shipyard worker-turned-hairdresser Brian Drumm, who, in the early 1980s, had the clever idea of putting a spirit level in an old-fashioned barber's comb. This simple addition made it easier to ensure that the fashionable retro rockabilly styles of the time could be cut perfectly straight. With the help of an ex-work colleague, Drumm produced the first version of what he called the 'Flat-topper' in a garage. But with an upmarket salon in Edinburgh and a client list including Princess Margaret, Simple Minds and the Bay City Rollers, Drumm seized an opportunity to turn his tool into a design icon.

"I heard that the Scottish Design Council were giving grants and I thought it was time to recreate the Flat-topper," says Drumm. The scheme led him to a young design team from London – Jonathan Ive and Martin Darbyshire at tangerine.

In one of his very first commercial projects, Ive produced a series of designs that embedded the spirit level between mouldings. The man who would go on to become the world-renowned head of design at Apple had taken Drumm's comb and given it an Ive make-over.

"The new Flatliner, as we called it, just looked absolutely beautiful," Darbyshire remembers, "and crucially it could be manufactured at a reasonably low cost." The design Drumm chose was, according to Darbyshire, by far the most complicated to produce, but was also the one that is quite recognisable even now as having been designed by Ive. "There is an essential elegance to it that is quite striking, and it is very clever in its use of form. It looks like a beautiful hand with fingers." Incorporating Drumm's spirit level within Ive's refined and stylish design created an object that had the qualities of a precision tool without the price tag.

With the concept created, Darbyshire then took over to see through the engineering challenge. "What I needed to do was to ensure that the mouldings fitted together perfectly with no visible fastenings, but this was in the days before most people, and certainly tangerine, could afford three-dimensional computer-aided design. So we made models in white foam."

"It was a fantastic thing and we made it ourselves," Drumm recalls. "First and foremost it was a tool – a tool to sculpt with." The comb couldn't just look good, it needed to feel good in the hand and have a natural balance. With the help of toolmakers, the duo from tangerine perfected a product that was inexpensive to produce but looked a million dollars.

Brian Drumm was immediately taken with the result. "When I saw the design, the lines of it, it was exactly what I wanted," he says. The Flatliner won the prestigious iF Product Design award in 1995 and remains in use in salons across the world.

More than 20 years after they first worked together, Darbyshire was astonished to hear from Drumm that more than two million of both versions have now been sold. The Edinburgh hairdresser was equally amazed to learn that the young man who sketched out designs for his comb had gone on to create some of the most iconic products ever made.

Left: The original Flat-topper single piece comb with snap-fit spirit level, designed by Brian Drumm.

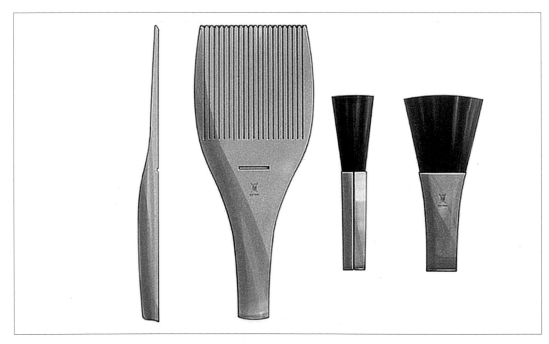

Left: The selected hand-drawn concept sketch for the Flatliner and associated brush.

Below left: One of a range of foam models made to resolve the 3D shape of the top and bottom mouldings that form the new comb.

Below: The Flatliner Comb in use.

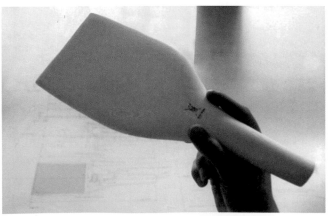

"...inexpensive to produce but looked a million dollars."

Right: Front view of the production Flatliner comb. The introduction of a two-piece construction, encapsulating the spirit level, gave a far more precise form to the viewing window. The two parts were designed to have a perfect fit along the flowing curve in the side view, enabling a change in the draft angle and a shape that sits comfortably in the hand.

02

Classic design possesses a calm,
self-evident authority that belies
the sweat and the guts needed
even to get close to it.

Mutant ninja toilets

Ideal Standard | 1990

Almost everyone in Britain will have had a meeting with Michelangelo in a toilet. The archetypal Renaissance man gave his name to perhaps the most ubiquitous range of bathroom ceramics in UK homes. But in the early 90s the manufacturer Ideal Standard had a plan to replace an ageing Michelangelo with a new model. This is the story of how a potential classic from one of the world's most celebrated designers ended up down the plughole.

Ideal Standard was always on the lookout for the next generation of design talent and, having spotted his work at a degree show in Newcastle, one of their scouts was keeping tabs on Jonathan Ive. By the time they were considering replacing the Michelangelo range, Ive had joined Martin Darbyshire and Clive Grinyer as a partner at tangerine. Ideal Standard threw down a challenge to the three designers: create a contemporary bathroom concept with mass appeal.

Ceramics present a peculiar design problem. According to Darbyshire, the firing process has a habit of turning the most brilliant ideas into a soggy mess. "You are forever having to throw away attempts that have sagged or drooped in the kiln," he says. "The material briefly becomes liquid as it changes from a semi-solid to solid state, which can alter the shape entirely."

Left: White foam model of the basin and pedestal of the Raphael concept.

Below: The original Michelangelo range, still sold under the Conca brand name in Italy.

Left: Raphael had subtle curves on the side and a flat back, allowing the pedestal to be fired on a flat surface, yet retain the curved shape.

Above, left to right: Further images of the original white foam model for the Raphael, Leonardo and Donatello concepts.

Below: Scale line-drawings of Raphael, Leonardo and Donatello basins and pedestals.

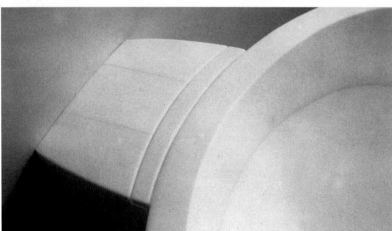

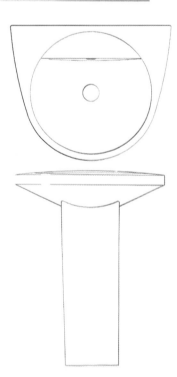

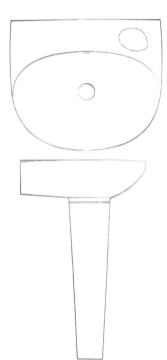

Above: Full-sized white foam model of the Leonardo toilet.

Below: Development sketch of the Raphael concept to show the basin being integrated with the pedestal in a one-piece solution.

"Hindsight is a powerful thing, but foresight takes courage. They missed out on a classic."

Martin Darbyshire

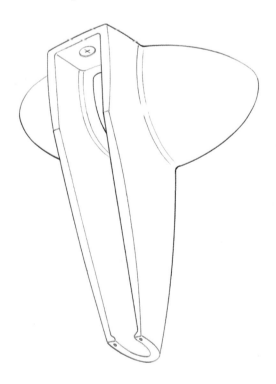

It was the shape-changing characteristics of ceramic coupled with the ghost of Michelangelo, perhaps, that saw the tangerine trio seek inspiration from the anthropomorphic Teenage Mutant Ninja Turtles. Like the cult cartoon characters, their three design concepts were named Raphael, Donatello and Leonardo.

"We didn't have any money and there weren't many good modelling services available," remembers tangerine founding partner Grinyer. "So we decided to decamp from Hoxton down to Jonathan's parents' house in Somerset." Deep in the English countryside, the three designers each worked on their own concept for a mass-produced bathroom suite. Days of cutting and shaping and laminating and sanding went by. "It was an incredibly disciplined process, but Jonathan in particular absolutely loved it," says Darbyshire. "He was in his element."

Three distinct concepts took shape, each in its own design language. "Donatello and Leonardo were pretty good," Darbyshire recalls, "and then there was Jonathan's – Raphael!" Ive's vision for a contemporary bathroom was, in Darbyshire's phrase, "predictably beautiful". The lines of the basin took inspiration from the scooping of liquid, the bowl an idealised attempt to capture the precious nature of water. "It had very subtle curves on the side but a flat back so you could fire the pedestal on a flat surface and still keep the curved shape," Darbyshire notes. "The challenge with the bowl, though, was that it needed to be fired twice. To change that would have ruined the design."

With full-size mock-ups of their basins and side views of their toilets finally completed, the three men excitedly packed their car and drove up to Hull for a meeting that has since entered design folklore.

The clown accessory might have been a clue to how things were going to go. It was the very early days of Comic Relief and, as they unpacked their prototypes, the young designers couldn't help but notice that Ideal Standard's Managing Director Roger Cooper was sporting a bright red plastic nose.

Product Manager Paul Frankish remembers the meeting as friendly and animated. "We immediately recognised the quality of what Ive had produced," he says. "It was incredibly innovative and ahead of its time." But perhaps it was too ahead of its time. "We could see it was refined, had naturally flowing lines and was very well integrated," Frankish recalls. "We just didn't think it would manufacture well."

Grinyer still believes the meeting exemplified a very British failure of imagination. "There was no desire to try and do something," he says. "If it had been an Italian company, they would have looked at it."

It was a rather subdued journey back to London. Ive had agreed to try to adjust his design, but in their hearts they all knew Raphael was dead. Darbyshire questions whether the problems were really so great they couldn't be overcome. "Hindsight is a powerful thing", he says, "but foresight takes courage. They missed out on a classic."

They also missed out on an association with a man who has become a design superstar. Shortly afterwards, encouraged by his partners at tangerine, Jonathan Ive took a plane to California and became the creative design genius behind the Apple empire. "We joke that it was Roger Cooper who launched the i-generation," Frankish says. "As soon as Ive went to Apple, we realised that Ideal Standard's loss was Apple's gain." Grinyer believes Ive was always destined to go to Apple, but "one of the straws that broke the camel's back" was a deep disappointment at the fate of his beautiful Raphael.

03

Design is misconceived as another word for style or flair or invention or even beauty. Design is a way of thinking, a philosophy that can be utterly transformative.

Korea break

LG Electronics | 1990–2014

If there is one business relationship that charts tangerine's development and evolving philosophy more than any other, it is with the giant Korean conglomerate LG. Across almost a quarter of a century and involving around 80 projects, it is an association that also mirrors the extraordinary development and changing philosophy of South Korea's relationship with design itself.

In 1990, as tangerine celebrated its first birthday, a new young partner joined the firm. Peter Phillips arrived with some useful contacts, including one relatively unknown in Europe – a large and ambitious Korean company specialising in household goods and electronics. "It was called Goldstar then and a very different company in those days," Phillips remembers. "Their major market was the Far East, but they were looking to expand into Europe and had set up an office in Dublin to try and get a European perspective on their products."

LG, as it later became, was also beginning to reassess the place and importance of design in its rapidly expanding business. "When tangerine first started working in Korea, design was generally regarded as a purely artistic discipline," says Professor Kun-Pyo Lee. The former Executive Vice-President and Design Centre Chief at LG is one of the country's most distinguished design academics. "Korean companies had really good technology, but they would just invite designers in later and ask them to make a product look different."

LG Vice-President and design expert Youngho Kim echoes the point. "In those early years, product design tended to be used as a 'styling', just wrapping products in nice shapes and pretty colours," he says. "Then we started to be interested in European design, which was mature, simple and concise in look and feel."

Product design in Korea was increasingly recognised as a vital part of business strategy. Companies like LG were eager to understand and exploit Western design expertise as they expanded into the European market. "I think they saw us as young, dynamic and not too expensive," Phillips recalls. "We developed a great relationship with their directors and they were a very loyal bunch." For a fledgling design company, LG was the ideal client.

Left: Production sample of LG's European 2012 fridge freezer. The dark vertical stripe was created to make the product distinctive in a crowded market.

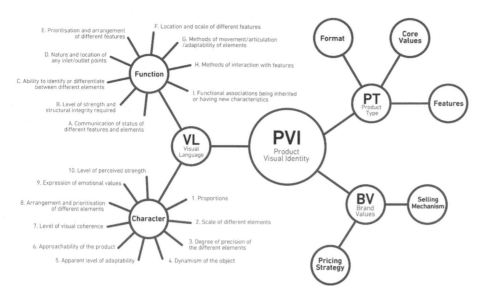

E. Prioritisation and arrangement of different features

F. Location and scale of different features

G. Methods of movement/articulation /adaptability of elements

D. Nature and location of any inlet/outlet points

H. Methods of interaction with features

C. Ability to identify or differentiate between different elements

I. Functional associations being inherited or having new characteristics

B. Level of strength and structural integrity required

A. Communication of status of different features and elements

Function

Format

Core Values

PT
Product Type

Features

VL
Visual Language

PVI
Product Visual Identity

10. Level of perceived strength

9. Expression of emotional values

8. Arrangement and prioritisation of different elements

7. Level of visual coherence

6. Approachability of the product

5. Apparent level of adaptability

Character

1. Proportions

2. Scale of different elements

3. Degree of precision of the different elements

4. Dynamism of the object

BV
Brand Values

Selling Mechanism

Pricing Strategy

Left: Product Visual Identity work mapped across three distinct areas; visual language, product type and brand value. The PVI creates a design language that can connect and give coherence to a wide range of products, within a category and across categories.

Below: This VCR for LG introduced a theatrical narrative.

"The connection has been a massive benefit for us, but also, I think, for them," says tangerine CEO Martin Darbyshire. "In business and in design, LG were determined to be winners. We believed we had the skills in both categories to help them in that ambition."

Youngho Kim remembers LG's thirst for new creative thinking at that time. "The role of an out-sourced design team like tangerine was to stimulate, to introduce new cultural ideas, to approach projects in a new way with a fresh mind," he says. "We needed to get out of our rut of old habits."

A wide range of LG projects came tangerine's way; everything from mobile phones to televisions, fax machines and refrigerators. The challenge for the London design team was to give each product some 'personality' compared to others in the market. "Before tangerine got involved there was no story with any of the products," says designer David Tonge, who took on a video recorder and a fax machine. "The design was just about packaging the technology. For tangerine, there had to be a story."

Tonge took LG's standard black VCR box and introduced a theatrical narrative. "The door was ribbed to make it look like a safety curtain and the sides had a slight curvature, which were like the pillars of a theatre stage," says Tonge. "With the fax machine, rather than being just a square block, it was about the story of a piece of paper gracefully moving."

Such an approach was a revelation to LG. "Co-working with tangerine, we started to break away from functional design to emotional design," Youngho Kim explains. "We began to focus much more on the user's perspective than the product styling."

LG had realised that an understanding of the European consumer was going to be critical for their plans to expand into Western markets. "How do you design a vacuum cleaner that is distinctive and helps LG get it right in Europe?" Darbyshire asks. "That was one challenge the client set us." tangerine embarked on a programme of detailed consumer research, interviewing and observing shoppers in three European countries. The trend at the time was to rely on focus groups or Hall tests to examine the user experience.

"The trouble with focus groups is that they tend to dwell on the negatives," Darbyshire says. "They can tell you what people don't like, but they cannot help you identify what consumers would like but haven't

"In those early years, product design tended to be used as a 'styling', just wrapping products in nice shapes and pretty colours."
Youngho Kim, Vice-President, LG

"The trouble with focus groups is that they tend to dwell on the negatives, they can tell you what people don't like but they cannot help you identify what consumers would like but haven't realized yet."
Martin Darbyshire

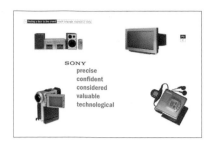

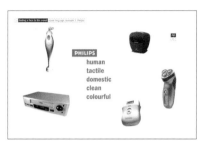

Above: Competitors' product values were examined to help give LG clarity on how to create a clear identity for their products.

Right: Cylinder vacuum cleaner designed as part of the strategy to help LG enter the European market.

Below, left to right: Video recorder, television and mini hi-fi, developed as part of the PVI strategy.

Left: Production sample of LG's European Fridge Freezer 2012, showing the very dark vertical stripe created to make the product distinctive in a crowded market.

Above: A range of concept designs developed in response to ethnographic, market and cultural research conducted across the UK, Spain and Germany. It reveals different approaches to both visual language and product features.

"Co-working with tangerine, we started to break away from functional design to emotional design. We began to focus much more on the user's perspective than the product styling."

Youngho Kim, Vice-President, LG

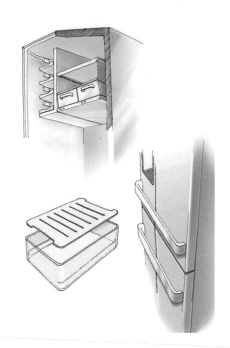

Above: Examples of product features and interior layouts created as a result of the European research.

realised yet, the unarticulated needs that move a brand forward. What we identified is that while a vacuum cleaner in Korea is a bit of a toy, a novelty thing to some extent, for a European it's a vital tool," he continues. "In Europe, it's also what's called a 'distress purchase' – you only replace your vacuum cleaner when your old one breaks and you need an urgent replacement. People tend not to research before they buy."

Such consumer insight enabled Matt Round, in his first project for tangerine in 1996, to fashion a product that looked and felt friendly, but was also robust and distinctive. "We came up with a machine that was easy to use, with simple, elegant features," Round explains. "Our original design was totally different to what a vacuum cleaner looked like in Korea."

It was a similar story with refrigerators. "Korean fridges are getting bigger with lots of gadgets and displays, but European fridges are much simpler," Professor Kun-Pyo Lee says. "This is an important distinction for us to understand, so the user experience is a core element of our design approach."

By no means all of tangerine's designs for LG in those early years made it through to market. With input from other outside agencies and an ever-increasing in-house design team at LG, other products represented an amalgam of ideas – results that, at times, disappointed Martin Darbyshire.

But LG were impressed enough by tangerine's approach to ask the British design company to help develop a strategy for their corporate design language in 1997. "They were aware that in Europe people didn't rate their brand, even though they had some very good technologies," says a former Creative Director at tangerine, Mike Woods. "Because of the trust we had built up doing everything from vacuums to videos with them, we were asked to do this project."

Woods began work on a 'design language' or Product Visual Identity that the Korean giant's in-house design team could utilise. "We tried to create a family feel, a DNA that would run through their products, so that the video recorder and the TV felt as though they were related," he recalls.

"The challenge is how you make that applicable to different countries, markets, positions and price entry levels," says Martin Darbyshire. "It's all about clarity of vision. The one thing designers hate is being told what to do, so the approach needed to inspire not prescribe."

As tangerine worked to help LG articulate their brand language in 1998, a fresh-faced design graduate from the Royal College of Art walked through the door of the office for a summer internship. Don Tae Lee told them he was Korean and was set to work on a project for LG. It quickly became obvious that this young man brought more than an excellent design portfolio.

"We already had a strong relationship with LG, but it really took off when Don arrived," Martin Darbyshire remembers. Now tangerine's President, Don went on to set up the company's Seoul office in 2004, allowing him to work directly with LG and other Korean clients. Ten years later the office is thriving and Don is particularly pleased with the continuing relationship with LG and the other Korean multinationals.

"Big projects often require joint input from London and Seoul. Korean companies can be very conservative and the culture is very different, which means it is not always easy to communicate and get ideas across," Don explains.

Acting as design and cultural interpreter, Don helped Korean business philosophy successfully mesh with tangerine's creative thinking. One project which exemplified the potential of such co-operation was an LG project for that most functional of objects, an air conditioning unit.

Professor Kun-Pyo Lee is effusive. "What a brilliant idea, what an achievement!" he says. "The Art Cool picture air conditioning unit has completely changed the concept of what was just a utilitarian product."

Martin Darbyshire explains the idea. "Most air-con units tend to be long skinny things that just get put up on the wall in the corner of the room where the pipes come in," he says. "What we did was design a square unit in the form of a picture frame into which the customer can put any picture they like."

The units have really caught the imagination of consumers in both Europe and the Far East. Hundreds of thousands have already been sold and new models are in development.

One product ever present in the long relationship between tangerine and LG has been the mobile phone – more than 20 projects in all.

"I was particularly impressed by the collaboration we did with the Cion EZ folder," Youngho Kim remembers. The product was a best-seller in 1999, but he and tangerine agree the mobile market is now completely different. Where once there would have been dozens of new handsets launched in a single year, today the focus has changed. "To beat the best products that are out there in the market, you have to create something exceptional," says Don. "You can't create 20 products and launch them all. What you are looking for now is one iconic design, a single strong concept."

During their time working together, tangerine and LG have seen their companies mature and evolve. The Korean giant now has 650 in-house designers in five offices around the world with a stated philosophy to focus on user experience. The British design house has built an enviable reputation for working successfully with clients in the Far East.

It has been a relationship that has shaped the business and the philosophy of both.

"The Art Cool picture air conditioning unit has completely changed the concept of what was just a utilitarian product."
Professor Kun-Pyo Lee, former LG Executive Vice-President and Design Centre Chief

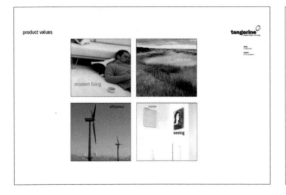

Above: The Art Cool air conditioning unit.

Left: Image boards and concept sketches of the Art Cool air conditioning unit; one of LG's most successful products.

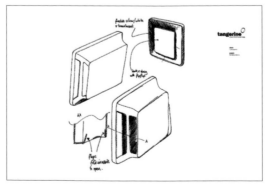

Right: Appearance model of the folder phone that inspired the design of one of LG's most successful mobiles, the Cion EZ folder.

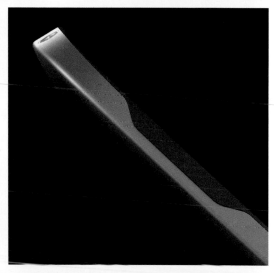

Above: Rear and top view of the coordinating smart phone.

Above Right: A detail of the edge profile and integrated controls of the tablet from the 'Smart Devices' project; the design of a new tablet with coordinating smart phone concept.

Right: Comparison between the outer profile of the tablet concept and the market-leading product.

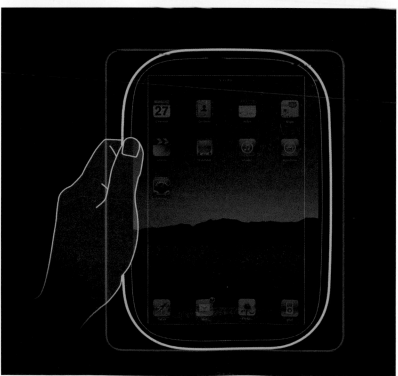

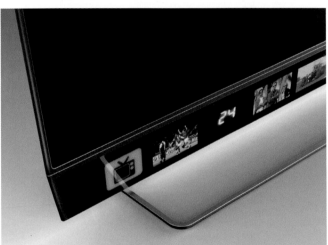

Above: Concept design for an LED TV that formed part of a major programme exploring how home entertainment and televisions would become integrated in the future. A key issue was the possibility of a second screen enabling off-screen navigation.

Left and below: The TV design under development in a series of models and computer renderings.

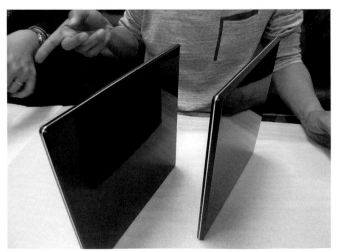

Below: Concept showing two potential directions for the next generation of Cyking vacuum cleaners. New technological developments for the dust extraction cylinder are explored together with a fresh approach to the visual language.

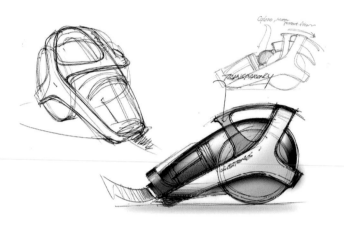

04

True innovation is often buried
in the most inaccessible places.
Courage, collaboration and
perseverance are required to
unearth it.

When the pressure gets too much

Novamedix | 1993

Brilliant design is about thinking big and thinking small. It is about grand ambition but also attention to detail. This is the tale of a design project that taught tangerine some vital lessons on how to achieve both. "It is a powerful story because it covered the whole spectrum", says tangerine CEO Martin Darbyshire. "It was a steep learning curve and we made some mistakes – but thankfully it worked in the end."

In the early 90s, Novamedix was a tiny company with a patent for a great product based on a UK medical discovery – a piece of equipment that improved the blood flow of immobile hospital patients without the need for drugs. The machine rapidly inflated a shoe placed around a patient's foot, the pressure shooting the blood up the legs to the heart and mimicking the vital job the feet and legs do all the time for people who are mobile. "The first production model of the A-V impulse system was a good solid bit of kit," the company MD Paul Gregory recalls, "but desperately in need of updating. The potential market, particularly in the US if we got it right, was huge."

"What they had was a relatively crude box with dials on the front, a power supply and some controlling electronics," Darbyshire says. "At that stage we were talking about what was basically a styling job. We were just discussing how to make the machine easier to use and better-looking."

"The design brief followed an extensive consultation exercise with our distributors in the United States," Gregory explains. "We were responding to what we believed our clients wanted."

Even in those early meetings, however, there were hints that the project might deliver a lot more. Darbyshire remembers looking at the product and thinking that this was a box that had no intelligence. "You just set it and that was it," he says. "I think Novamedix had no concept of how far they could take it and, I must admit, at that point in time neither did we."

Like Novamedix, tangerine was also a small company at the time, but Gregory was convinced the young agency was perfect for the contract. "I can smell bullshit at a thousand paces, so I knew these were serious people with design savvy," he says. "Their portfolio was relatively limited, but that was part of the attraction – they didn't come steeped in years of how medical devices should be done."

Left: Production sample of the Novamedix A-V impulse system.

Above: Original unit.

"To this day, it is an object lesson in how to make things user-friendly,"

Paul Gregory, Managing Director

Aware of their lack of experience in the medical technology field, Darbyshire brought in electronics consultant Tim Frost, a man he describes as "a complete whizz with software". Frost's arrival meant the project team was able to open their minds to what could be achieved. They could start to think big. Frost set to work on giving the dumb machine some brains. "Patients may kink the hose or the pressure may need to be adapted as conditions change, but the original machine couldn't react to things like that," Frost says. "I suggested using a micro-controller so it can detect what's going on and we can actually make it function a lot better."

Meanwhile, tangerine and Novamedix worked together on identifying ways to reduce the manufacturing cost of the machine, replacing expensive metal parts with cheaper moulded plastic alternatives. The tangerine designers were also looking to improve the user experience. For Frost, it would prove one of the most satisfying working relationships of his career. "The fact they were coming at it from a different angle and that their interest was visual, I found very stimulating," he says. "It's like all design. If you just have a blank sheet of paper and do your own thing, it's OK. But if you have to react to other people it sparks a bit more, like the grit and the oyster that produce the pearl."

"tangerine suggested this organic, feminine shape rather than the masculine hard-edged square box we had," says Gregory. "Patients have to interact with this device, so making it a human-looking product was an important part of the design." They also redesigned the LCD display so users would intuitively understand what was happening. Pictograms meant the machine was easy to use, whatever the language of staff or patients.

"To this day, it is an object lesson in how to make things user-friendly," Gregory reckons. "The graphics and the way the information was presented were extremely clever." The designers had been thinking about the smallest details.

In many ways, the project was a good example of how combining grand ambition and attention to detail produced a product that proved a huge commercial success. The machine is still manufactured to this day and has helped treat in excess of 20 million patients worldwide. But those involved also remember it for an important lesson on what not to do.

Within the device is a vessel where air pressure builds up and is then released down tubes to inflate the slipper on the patient's foot. "The old model had a tank made from aluminium that would last from here to eternity – it was bomb-proof," Gregory explains. "With the new model, we agreed to mould the pressure vessel in plastic to reduce substantially production costs." With Novamedix anxious to get the product to market quickly, tangerine took the word of the plastics manufacturer that the material would be up to the job. "We were working outside of our experience a bit," Darbyshire admits. "We made mistakes in not checking the pressure vessel ourselves, but Novamedix also launched it very fast."

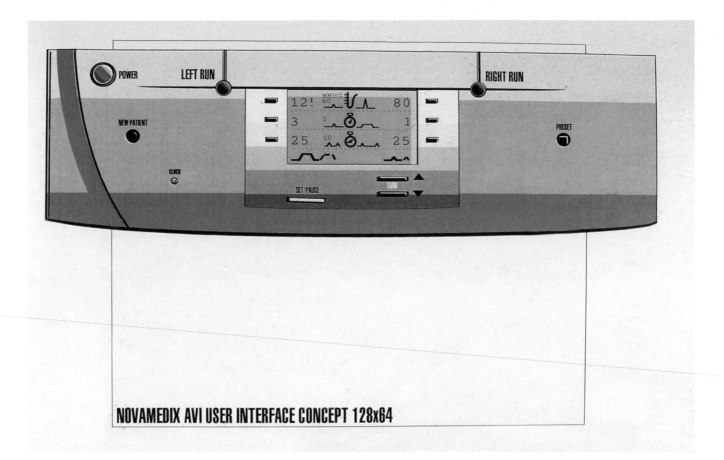

NOVAMEDIX AVI USER INTERFACE CONCEPT 128x64

Above: Early hand-drawn concept sketch showing the custom-designed LCD display.

Right: The production LCD display showing:
1) the machine first running normally;
and
2) indicating a fault with a kink in the hose.
The happy/sad face icons make it easy to understand whether the machine is functioning correctly or needs assistance.

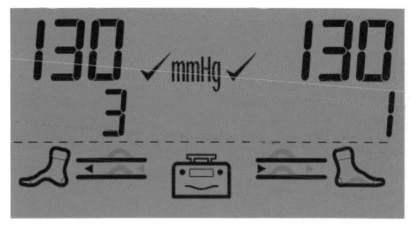

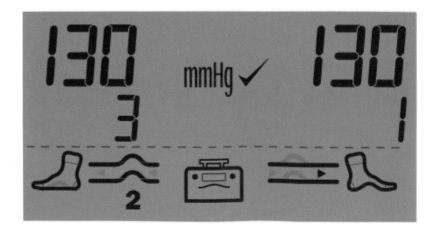

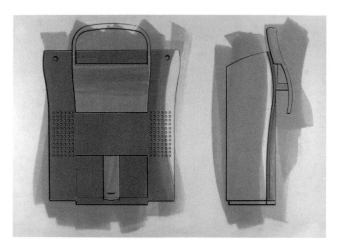

Above: The initial concept was designed to reflect a torso and express powerful exhaling. Hand-drawn sketches show details of the side and rear of the unit.

Right: The first foam model showing the detailing of the hand-drawn sketch.

Below: First appearance model accurately representing the size of the production unit. It was constructed following the initial engineering development work.

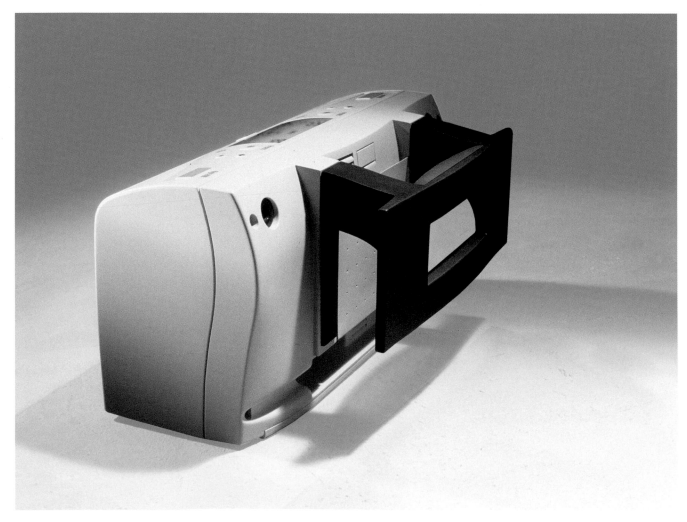

After the product reached the market, some pressure tanks started to crack and split open. "When the first few failed, we did a heap of testing and realised the fatigue life on these things was much shorter than we'd envisaged," says Gregory. It was decided that, rather than recall the devices, customers would all be offered a free upgrade and regular servicing while Darbyshire worked with Novamedix engineers to put the problem right. "It was a very painful and expensive six months," Darbyshire says. "We found another company who could do more detailed stress analysis and help solve the problem. We made modifications to the tooling and the Novamedix engineering manager did an amazing amount of work developing the technique to join the tank parts together."

But despite the discomfort and the cost, all those involved still remember the project fondly. "We learned some really important lessons," Darbyshire says. "We also created a product which to this day means millions of people have an alternative to medication – which is a really massive benefit."

Below: First production sample showing all of the internal components, including the pressure vessel and controlling electronics, the customised LCD and the switch-mode power supply.

05

It is a gift to be blessed with
eyes that see beyond the horizon;
success belongs to those who
survey the future from all angles.

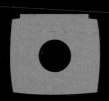

A blinkin' good idea

Blink | 1994

Designers often complain that constraints put on them by clients inhibit creativity. So what happens if a design team dreams up its own concept with no thought of the end market? This is the story of one such rare creature.

In the early days of tangerine, CEO Martin Darbyshire wanted to make a statement about tangerine's approach to design. "Most of our competitors were obsessed with concurrent engineering at that time," he says. "I wanted to show what can happen when you stand back and really think about a product, look at how applicable it is and how it might develop in the future."

An international competition to find products for an ageing population offered the perfect excuse. Darbyshire asked designer Heather Martin, fresh out of university, to work on a project that would rethink the traditional point-and-shoot camera for older people. "It was a great project for me," Heather says. "Up to that point, I had been working on standard microwaves and televisions and remotes, so this was very different and it was nice to do something that was pushing things to where the future was going."

The idea was to take the analogue camera into the digital age. "At that time, people were still using SLR or disposable cameras," Darbyshire recalls. "Film was still dominant." The tangerine designers challenged themselves to harness the very latest technology for people who were frightened by technology.

"Because we were designing for an older population, we didn't think it made any sense that people with fading eyesight would have to hold the camera up to their eyes to take photos through a tiny little window," Heather explains. "So, I said why don't we put an LCD on the back so they can look at the image from a distance and see what they are taking."

It was the first time a hand-held camera had incorporated an LCD display. But there were other aspects of the camera – christened 'Blink' – that were years ahead of their time. "Instead of having a film cartridge in the camera, we incorporated a solid-state, digital, storage device," says Heather. "It contained the photographs, and you popped it out of the camera and slotted it into a square viewing machine."

Long before such ideas became mass market, Blink had a digital memory card that could be inserted into a digital photo frame. Despite

Left: As digital technology was emerging, the Blink concept camera and photo file identified a system that could do more than just take photographs and store them.

Right: The Blink system offered the potential to transfer files via the digital storage cassette onto the photo frame. The pictures could then be viewed, manuipulated and filed away. It featured simple controls like the open and close shutter doors that also switched the camera on and off. These features, explored in 1994, are now commonplace, showing that good design can predict the future.

Below: The prize-winning Blink was designed for the Shinanogawa Technopolis Design Competition at the 1994 International Design Fair in Nagoya, Japan.

the novelty, the aim was always to make the technology as user-friendly as possible. "The camera had a pair of large sliding shutters that you slid back like a pair of doors," Darbyshire explains. "As soon as you did that, you switched the camera on, so you didn't have to worry about hunting for a power button."

"On the viewer, there was software that allowed users to crop, so even if they hadn't done a good job, they could easily reposition or crop by using the photo-touch screen," Heather says. "There was also a touchpad where you could just run your thumb over and it would flick through the images like a photo-album."

Here, too, the Blink digital system can be seen as a pioneer of ideas and technology that would not hit the shelves for years. It was also a product sculpted to appeal to particular users. "We were trying to get away from a camera being masculine – a black, square-looking object," Heather reveals. "We wanted to soften it up by introducing a double curvature on the front surface, so it felt nice to hold."

tangerine took their ideas to top model-maker Chris Hill of Solve 3D. "I've been involved in making thousands of models and a good number for tangerine, but I remember Blink because it was so unusual," Hill says. "There were sketches from which we worked on handmade models." Blink, he admits, was one of his models that he found it hard to let out of the door. "tangerine expected the best and this was a very important project because it reflected the true state of model-making at the time."

The camera was not like anything on the market at that time. "Nowadays everything has LCDs and touch screens. Devices allow you to run your finger across like a book," Heather says. "That's all happened in the last five years, but this was 20 years ago."

For Darbyshire, the Blink project was about demonstrating what tangerine was about. "We were trying to use this to show how our philosophy focused on the end user," he says, "how our designs could be distinctive and appropriate, applying technology in a more interesting, engaging and meaningful way."

The camera and viewer were highly commended in the competition but never marketed. That wasn't the point. As Heather puts it, "Blink was designed to stimulate people to ask a question: Why aren't we doing things like this?"

"Nowadays everything has LCDs and touch screens. Devices allow you to run your finger across like a book. That's all happened in the last five years, but this was 20 years ago."
Heather Martin

06

When format and form are the defining qualities of a market, imaginative design can be the driving force in reaching new business.

Beauty in the third dimension

GCS mobile and cordless phones | 1995

In London in the mid-90s, there was hardly a product design house that wasn't thinking mobile phones. It was early days for the technology, but the challenge then was much as it is today: how to take virtually standard internal components and bless them with character and beauty.

"They were all quite large, key-based phones in those days, of course," says David Tonge, a designer at tangerine at the time. "The one we were working on in this project was pretty slim compared to others, but it still had a big antenna on it."

The basic device may have been familiar, but a very different client had come calling. "We opened the door and an extraordinary white-haired character called Bill White walked in," remembers tangerine CEO Martin Darbyshire. "He said he wanted us to design the first ever GSM phone for his company, GCS." "He was very charismatic, very energetic, a real character," says Tonge. "Bill was the kind of client who was very hands on! Dealing with him was interesting."

Tonge, who had been introduced to tangerine by Jonathan Ive, was intrigued to find the client sitting in on every design session. "It's exactly what you don't want normally," Tonge says, "but some of Bill's energy rubbed off on the project. You have very little to work on, but you need to get something in there and give it some personality compared to other products in the market place."

tangerine wanted to find an extra dimension in the design process, quite literally. "At that time, a lot of products were designed from the front," says Darbyshire. "It usually began as a two-dimensional process, pencil on paper, then progressed rapidly to physical models, all handmade at the time."

Tonge decided to take his hand-sketched and sophisticated shapes to model maker, Chris Hill of Solve 3D. "We all sat in a room together, model makers and designers, and we would brainstorm how to achieve the required shapes, translating from 2D elevation views into coherent models," Hill remembers. Darbyshire recalls that this was the very early days of 3D computer-aided design, "so the next stage was to create all the data and surface-model all the plastics using 3D CAD. The result was something considerably slimmer and less blocky than anything around at the time."

Left: Appearance model of the GCS DECT (one of the first digital cordless handsets), which aimed to create simple elegant form and usage.

Below: Initial hand-drawn concept sketches of the two preferred directions for the GCS GSM mobile, subsequently built as appearance models. Both were quite radical for the time.

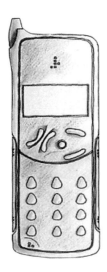

"The big thing we did," says Tonge, "was to add some shape – simple curvature, although it had to be very subtle. If you want to add shape of any kind, you will be adding volume."

Bill White went away a happy man, but soon he was back asking tangerine to work on other projects for GCS – and this time he stayed out of the design meetings. "GCS just wanted great-looking objects," says Mike Woods, a former creative director who led the design team. "We didn't have to negotiate with engineers at the beginning, it was all about trying to make something really beautiful."

The DECT handset was at the cutting edge of technology at the time, with a dock that allowed the user to walk around without a cable attached to the phone. But Bill White wanted tangerine to give his company's DECT device some soul. Once again, he was not disappointed. "Yes, it did have soul," Woods says. "It had a natural elegance and didn't look like it was trying too hard to be overtly designed. Yet every single surface and part had been agonised over to sculpt a really beautiful form."

The handset went from a subtle convex curvature to a subtle concave. "It had a kind of visual tension to it," enthuses Woods. "You pour your heart and soul into making this thing right and that's where the soul of product design comes from. At the time you are doing it, it's the only thing that matters."

"It had a natural elegance and didn't look like it was trying too hard to be overtly designed. Yet every single surface and part had been agonised over to sculpt a really beautiful form."
Mike Woods

Left: Hand-made appearance models of the GCS Slimline GSM, the form of which was difficult to resolve between 2D data and 3D form.

Neither phone actually quite made it to production – problems with the roaming software in the GSM handset, rather than any weakness in design. But they did create a stir in the shows they were shown in. Woods and Darbyshire drove them across Europe themselves to the highly prestigious CeBit show in Hanover to display them. "We looked around at the huge stands, all beautifully designed, and realised the scale of the challenge for a company like GCS competing with the big boys," says Darbyshire. "But the products punched way above their weight and enabled GCS to really stand out and attract potential customers."

At the Design Show in London, the prototypes helped the team win new business. Manfred Hubert, then Design Director at the giant French Groupe SEB, saw them and as a result tangerine went on to do a project with Rowenta. "Still now what I am sure about," says Hubert, "is that even in the 90s and before touch screens, the mobile was a good guide to design ability. It's not only a physical tool but also a communication one, carrying more potential dimensions which effective designers can play with."

For Darbyshire, though, the GCS designs fill him with pride for a different reason. "If you look at them now, there's still something quite new and appealing about them," he suggests. "It is quite rare to have something you can look back on like that, and still think it is beautiful and original, yet still fitting."

Right: Renderings of the GCS Slimline GSM handset. The data was modelled and rendered in Alias Wavefront to give excellent definition of the complex 3D surfaces.

07

Convention is the enemy of
invention, accepted wisdom
a crutch for lazy thinking.
Challenging preconception
is the source of all creativity.

Actively changing attitudes

Central Saint Martins | 1996

Gathering dust in cupboards and sheds across Britain are tens of thousands of abandoned walking frames. It is estimated that up to a third of Zimmers issued by the health service remain unused because elderly and disabled people think them hideous and medical.

"The very worst icon of disability is the Zimmer walking frame," a former Creative Director Mike Woods believes. "People would rather struggle on without them because they are seen as 'equipment' not 'product', designed for survival mode not living mode." So when tangerine was asked to work on a redesign, Woods jumped at the chance. "This was an opportunity to show what can be achieved when you think about what people want rather than what they need," Woods says.

Rethinking the Zimmer was part of the Design for Ability project, funded through Central Saint Martins School of Art and Design, which examined how disabled people felt stigmatized by devices designed to help them. "We wanted to treat disabled people just as you would any other group of consumers," says Design for Ability Director Malcolm Johnston. "For the first time, we brought in industrial designers and encouraged them to remove the dividing line between products for able-bodied and disabled people."

tangerine already had a close relationship with Central Saint Martins – Woods lectured to undergraduates, and CEO Martin Darbyshire was a visiting professor mentoring post-graduate students.

"I was struck by the waste of resources, handing out products that consumers don't want," Darbyshire recalls. "The manufacturing cost is kept to an absolute minimum, but if a large percentage end up under the stairs because people feel embarrassed and medicalised using them, then that's no benefit." Woods agrees. "Procurement in the NHS tends to go for the cheapest that gets the job done, but that masks the true cost if the stuff is not used," he says. "Better design and better understanding of users would lead to a better experience and would save money."

It was not going to be easy, however. "It's such a geometric nightmare," Woods concluded, after examining the classic NHS frame. "It is an awful thing to try to design because you have to get the support in the right place, the structure right and make it functional."

Left: The user's view of the ACTIV appearance model.

Left: A lifestyle board highlighting the choices of particular research subjects.

strident
intelligent
active
pessimistic
conservative

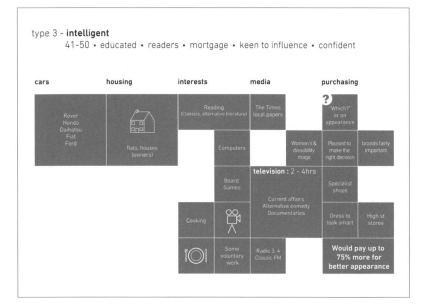

Below left: Maps of findings from psychographic profiling of the research subjects, helping the designers identify behaviour and aspirations.

type 3 - **intelligent**
    41-50 • educated • readers • mortgage • keen to influence • confident

cars	housing	interests	media		purchasing
					?
Rover Honda Daihatsu Fiat Ford		Reading (Classics, alternative literature)	The Times local papers		"Which?" or on appearance
	flats, houses (owners)	Computers		Women's & dissability mags	Pleased to make the right decision · brands fairly important
		Board Games	**television : 2 - 4hrs**		Specialist shops
		Cooking	Current affairs Alternative comedy Documentaries		Dress to look smart · High st stores
		Some voluntary work	Radio 3, 4 Classic FM		**Would pay up to 75% more for better appearance**

type 3 - **active**
    31-50 • educated • parents • mortgage • politically knowledgable • adventurous

cars	housing	interests	media		purchasing
			newspapers: Guardian the Mirror		**?**
		Reading (sci-fi)			"Which?"
	house, flats, bungalow (mortgages, renting)	Computers	Computers Magazines · Entertainment guides		informed decisions
Ford Austin Renault Peugeot Nissan		DIY gardening sports instruments	**television : 2 - 4hrs**		Sainsburys
			Educational Dr Who Detective series		Argos Littlewoods catalogues · John Lewis dept stores
		Art galleries Theatre	Radio 4 Classic FM		Brands fairly important

Above: The basic walking frame provided by the NHS.

He decided not to change the points where the frame touches the ground, or where the user grips it. Everything in between, though, was up for reconsideration. "We came up with five sketches for five different frames for five different people," Woods explains. "Each had its own visual language and functionality for distinct consumer groups."

Malcolm Johnston went to the tangerine studio and was impressed. "They didn't treat disabled people as one amorphous mass. They presented their different ideas and that always led to a stimulating discussion."

From the sketches and discussions, the first three-dimensional model emerged. "What was important was that the team were looking at the consumer from a lifestyle perspective rather than from the physiological nature of their disability," says Darbyshire.

Christened the 'ACTIV Walking Frame', the prototype was received enthusiastically at Central Saint Martins. "It was a brilliant job and a great design," says Johnston. "While the Zimmer frame relies on fixed components in a cage-like structure, the ACTIV has a strong joint and extending structure."

The more important evaluation, though, would come when the frame was unveiled to people who might actually use it. At the official launch in March 1998 was the first wheelchair user elected to Parliament, Dame Anne Begg MP. "It looked classy and sleek, not at all like the industrial-looking Zimmer frames," she remembers. "The frame passed the real test of whether a disability aid is a good design or not – someone without a disability said, 'I wish I had one.'"

Mike Woods remembers how physiotherapists came up to him at the event, asking where they could get the stylish walking frames. "Here was something designed for a distinct market which might actually become aspirational for the mainstream market."

The ACTIV was showcased in the British pavilion at Expo 2000 in Hanover, Germany. It was featured by Dame Tanni Grey-Thompson in *Does He Take Sugar?* on BBC Radio 4. It was discussed at the Design Council and the King's Fund in London. Five manufacturers expressed an interest in producing it commercially.

But it never got made.

"They just weren't brave enough to stick their necks out and go for it," Malcolm Johnston concludes. "Health service people loved the design, but it required a leap of faith which just wasn't there. There were concerns about cost constraints because the unit price has to be very low in the NHS."

Nevertheless, the project is seen as important in changing attitudes and thinking about disability aids. Dame Anne Begg believes "you can see its impact in many modern frames with seats used by older patients now, though sadly you can't get them on the NHS." Mike Woods reflects, "It probably had more influence than we realised."

"It looked classy and sleek, not at all like the industrial-looking Zimmer frames. The frame passed the real test of whether a disability aid is a good design or not – someone without a disability said, 'I wish I had one.'"
Dame Anne Begg MP

Left: One of a number of moodboards created for each of the five lifestyle categories identifed.

Below: An initial sketch book idea exploring form and features for a new frame.

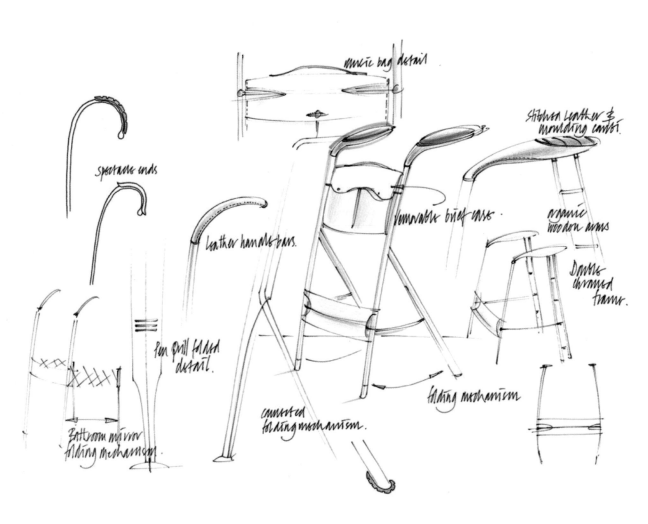

Right: Photos of the ACTIV walking frame in use. The table is deployed for extended tasks while standing and stowed away to enable movement.

08

Design should be seen, not as a cost but as an investment. There are always risks, but be bold and the rewards can be spectacular.

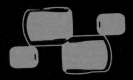

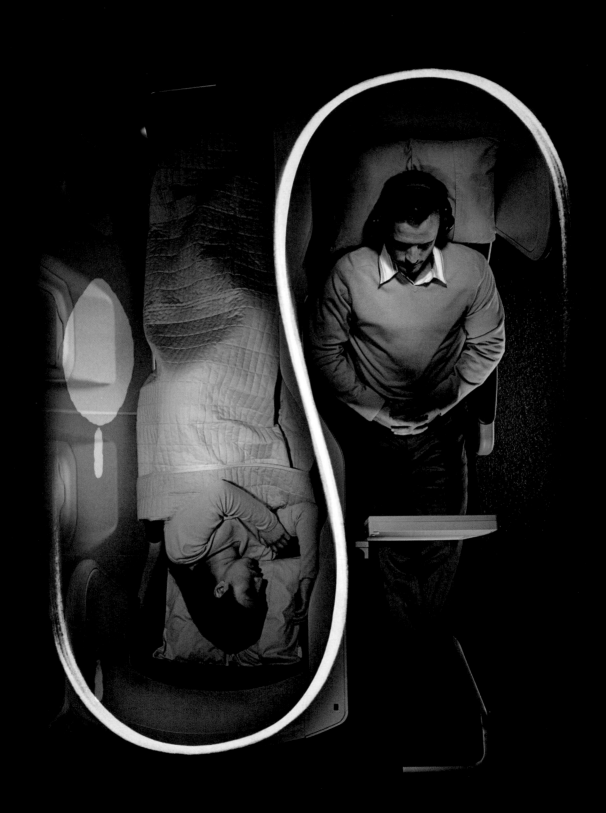

Working flat out for BA

British Airways | 1998–2014

At 32,000ft creativity and rigour are going to be tested to the limit. One needs to remain philosophical.

The challenge presented to tangerine by British Airways was daunting: "Find us the holy grail of airline travel sprinkled with a bit of pixie-dust – and astound us along the way." BA's Director of Marketing at the time, Martin George, says the airline wanted "something that was genuinely different and distinctive".

It was a turbulent time for the aviation industry: the global economy was lurching disconcertingly, fuel prices had begun to rise sharply and competition in the skies was increasingly fierce. Every major airline was scanning the horizon to locate the point of difference that would give them a business advantage.

The response from tangerine to the BA brief was "Project Dusk" – an audacious design solution that would stun the commercial aviation industry, redefine the business market and become the profit engine for British Airways. "It was something many regarded as simply impossible," says tangerine CEO Martin Darbyshire – nicknamed 'the Professor' by executives at BA because of his technical know-how. "We came up with a totally lie-flat bed in Business Class that kept the same number of seats while enhancing the very special BA brand."

It was a hard-won pitch involving the whole tangerine team, including Martin Darbyshire, Matt Round and Don Tae Lee.

For weeks, tangerine's Creative Director Matt Round had made the company offices resemble a dormitory after an earthquake: there were modelled beds everywhere and at every conceivable angle – slanted, end to end, side by side, on top of one another. "It's essential to have something physical to feel and make one aware of how spacious or cramped something feels," Round explains. "It is amazing how different things appear when they are physical and how dramatically they can shift your perceptions."

Project Dusk was about understanding the psychology of the business passenger as much as the practical constraints of an airliner. That became the focus of tangerine's and BA's approach. A sleep expert, recruited to advise tangerine, explained that the average person turns over 30 times a

Left: The current iconic Club World seat created by tangerine showing the yin-yang innovation symbol; the seat is still flying a decade-and-a-half after its first flight.

Below: The Club World cradle seat in use by BA until it was replaced in 2000 by the first version of the lie-flat bed. When introduced, the orginal seat was innovative and ahead of its time, but industry and customer expectations had moved on.

night. If you can't turn in your airline seat, you never reach the state of deep sleep necessary to arrive properly rested, they were told. And the key to turning over was lying flat.

Designers took flights to see what the current experience was like. "You look under every stone on the beach," says Darbyshire, "and always bear in mind the benefit to the person using it and to the business paying for it."

There wasn't a sudden eureka moment to the project, but the answer, when it came, was ground-breaking – the now world-famous and fully patented yin-yang approach. From the apparent chaos of Round's model beds emerged a formation that would redefine the design of aircraft interiors. Instead of all passengers facing the front of the cabin, seats were paired in a forward/rearward formation. "No one had ever considered arranging cabin space in this way," says Round.

The yin-yang approach allowed the design team to consider new and creative ways of using the fixed amount of cabin space: arm rests could be cleverly positioned over each other; the footstool could be separated from the seat to give passengers more freedom of movement and greater comfort; a lower, reclined seat geometry offered a more welcoming environment when boarding.

"Passengers told us they yearned for the freedom to move as they wished," Darbyshire explains. "This design allowed people to move around and feel special. We were offering a lounge in the sky."

The design team believed they had indeed uncovered something unique – a fully flat, six-foot bed in Business Class while still keeping eight seats abreast. Martin George remembers the moment when tangerine unveiled it to the airline's in-house team. "The reaction was wow!" he recalls. "People thought this is amazing. It could deliver the crown jewels – but I was actually very nervous. We had yet to convince the BA board."

It was a huge decision for the airline. Should they spend millions on an untried concept for their Business Class cabins at such an uncertain time for the industry? "It had never been done before, and it was a calculated risk with enormous implications," says George.

Experts from across BA's operation worked closely with tangerine to help get the project to fly. It was a testing time in more senses than one. The project team had to be confident the new seats were robust enough – any technical failure could have been disastrous. "On the New York route, for example, there would be 96 Club World seats," Darbyshire notes. "At 35,000ft [10,700m], you don't want them going wrong."

The design of any aircraft seat throws up unique challenges. Oxygen masks are in a fixed place above the seats in each cabin, but passengers lying down must still be able to reach them. The food table needs to be stored and seat-belts must function in all positions.

The yin-yang approach envisaged 'petal' dividers between the beds to provide a sense of privacy. But every seat still needed to offer crew access for service. A tangerine team worked with the manufacturers for five months as the first prototypes were produced, putting the seat through a wide range of dynamic tests. "It was testing for the seat but also for us," the Professor admits. "An intensively complex interaction of complicated parts had to come together in a seamless way."

However, it wasn't simply the engineering that had to be considered. Early research suggested some passengers might feel uncomfortable flying backwards – a psychological barrier to the yin-yang design. "My gut feeling

"Find us the holy grail of airline travel sprinkled with a bit of pixie-dust – and astound us along the way."
Martin George, former Director of Marketing, British Airways

"The reaction was wow! People thought this is amazing. It could deliver the crown jewels – but I was actually very nervous. We had yet to convince the BA board."
Martin George, former Director of Marketing, British Airways

Above: The 'lounge in the sky' concept. This set the vision for the yin-yang format, offering space efficiency and lie-flat beds. The passenger had increased privacy, greater comfort and the freedom to be themselves.

Right: Two of the early spatial models used to optimise seat size and define the positioning of its many elements, including tray table, video screen and footstool.

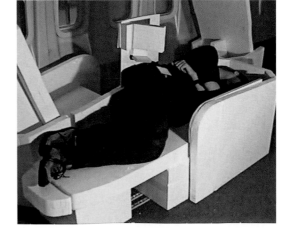

"You look under every stone on the beach and always bear in mind the benefit to the person using it and to the business paying for it."
Martin Darbyshire

was that it would work," Darbyshire recalls, "so BA proposed detailed research conducted in their lounges."

While they waited for the results of the survey, the tangerine team were taking to the skies themselves. Trial flights with the RAF were arranged to reassure the doubters that people wouldn't suffer motion sickness flying backwards. The exercise demonstrated that, unlike a car or a train where a passenger relates to the landscape outside, a large passenger aircraft is not close enough to anything for travel sickness to be a significant problem.

When the in-depth survey from British Airways' lounges had been collated, the results showed only one passenger in a hundred people was opposed to the idea of facing backwards, and they would have plenty of forward-facing seats to choose from. Yin-yang was still on the table. Everything now depended on convincing the BA board.

Martin George still remembers the trepidation mixed with excitement as he prepared to present Project Dusk to the airline's executives in the form of a foam mock-up model. "We'd done the research and then we just had to push it. Half a dozen of us walked the board through every detail."

There was nervousness, too, at tangerine, where everyone was waiting to hear the decision. At a launch ceremony in a London television studio, simultaneously released to the world via the Internet, Chief Executive Bob Ayling explained how the airline was basing its future on the results of extensive research into what frequent flyers said they wanted. "They want us to be the best in the world," he said. "So do we."

With a bold investment of £200 million, Project Dusk had dawned. In the autumn of 2000, yin-yang design would take to the skies. "It's the best thing our company has ever done," Ayling confided to tangerine.

Above: One of numerous rigs used to evaluate the height and angle of the seat and footstool with subjects ranging from the 5th to 95th percentile. This example was built on a rocking base and used to evaluate the comfort of rear-facing passengers during take-off.

Below: The Club World seat was the first lie-flat Business Class bed in the world. Another transformative innovation was the low and reclined seat position available immediately on boarding. Combined with a separate footstool, passengers could change posture easily and remain more comfortable over extended periods. Previously reclining chairs tend to lock the passenger into one posture, so reducing comfort.

Above: The concept was transformed into a full engineering design by close co-working with the seat manufacturer. Over a five-month period, 3D data of the exterior surfaces was compiled in parallel with the development of the seat mechanism engineering.

"A good client is important to the design process," says Matt Round. "They need to be able to delegate, but you also need champions to make things happen. Good design is balancing all the stakeholders; consumers, finance, marketing, engineering. Departments sometimes spend their time covering their backsides and end up with mediocrity."

Fifteen months from the beginning of the project, the first fitted plane was in the sky. As Round puts it, "pretty pacey by any standards". But Project Dusk was never rushed. "Looking for any quick result under pressure is not going to work. You have to have the space to play around."

BA's business customers also felt they had the space to play around. Passengers fell in love with the lounge in the sky. The cabin crew championed it. The board saw a return on their huge investment within 12 months. Shareholders were delighted that, by the time the whole fleet was fitted out, BA was profiting from it.

"People were choosing to fly British Airways," says Martin George. "Cabin crew were able to reassure those customers who'd been a bit worried about flying backwards and, in fact, we had passengers actually telling one another this is terrific."

The seat won the prestigious Design Business Association Grand Prix for design effectiveness and, less than a year after its launch, was given pride of place in the lobby of Miami's Museum of Contemporary Art.

"It is amongst the most innovative things the aviation industry has ever done and has changed the way the business world thinks about flying," says Round. "Prior to that, everyone was flying all night sat bolt upright. Now you wouldn't think of it."

The new Club World had set BA apart from all its competitors and redefined the Business Class experience for the whole industry.

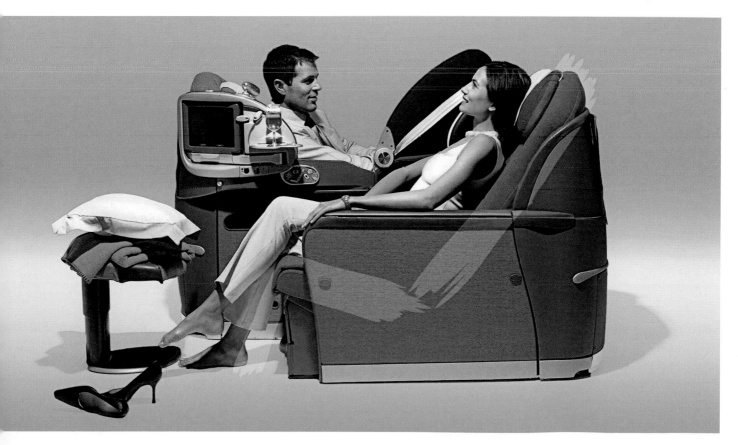

Left: The first production model of the Club World lie-flat bed.

"It's the best thing our company has ever done."
Bob Ayling former CEO, British Airways

Below: Plan and side-views illustrating the first- and second-generation Club World seats. In the second generation, angling the pair of seats at two degrees to the centre line of the aircraft and making the arms drop, made the bed 25 per cent wider within the same footprint.

Bottom: Plan views of both generations of seat showing how they still occupy the same footprint despite the second version's 25 per cent width increase.

1st Generation

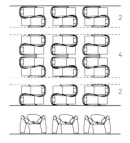

2nd Generation

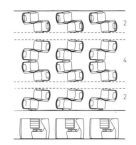

It was no surprise when, five years later, the time came to look again at Business Class cabins and British Airways went back to tangerine. Critically for the design team, the airline had agreed to go for a complete redesign rather than a straightforward upgrade.

Jamie Cassidy, who headed BA's long haul development at that time, likened the original tangerine bed "to a Swiss Army knife, containing a great deal of functionality in a small space. We wanted them to both increase functionality and capability of the original while restricting them from adding weight or reducing seat count." Cassidy admits he was sceptical of what could be achieved in "Project Stretch".

But success, it turned out, hinged on a matter of two degrees. By that tiny change to the angling of the seat, the designers were able to increase the width of the new flat bed by 25 per cent without any loss of seats in the cabin. The Professor was at it again.

"The Stretch design surpassed our expectations in terms of what was feasible or possible," says Cassidy. "Not only did it address all of the customer feedback within the confines of weight and seat count, it also changed the whole look and feel of the seat, making it more contemporary with much cleaner lines."

New materials and technology also saw a step-change in standards of well-being and privacy combined with safety. The design of the seat back and pan structure created by BE Aerospace delivered a new seat geometry, improving comfort when very reclined, and actually moving adjacent passengers a further 20cm (8in) apart. The use of Crystalflex diaphragms, also dramatically increased comfort levels.

Another example of technology and creativity combining to improve the passenger experience was the use of specially sourced translucent material in the screens between the seat and the aisle. This appears opaque to the passenger but clear for the cabin steward, thus allowing cabin service. An ingenious system for ensuring the screens lower in an emergency was also introduced. The electric pulse that drops the oxygen masks is used to 'switch off' the electromagnets in the screen mechanism, thus dropping it every time without fail. The Project Stretch team was still astounding people.

"The two versions of the seats are clever for different reasons," says Martin Darbyshire. "The second one answered the fundamental physics challenge of making something bigger in the same space."

It meant another massive investment for BA, but the re-fit essentially re-invented the Business Class experience for a second time. In 2012, seven years after it was introduced, BA flew almost 2.5 million Business Class customers and according to Jamie Cassidy, Club World "continues to be one of the world's most successful cabins."

"In a genuine partnership you create together what you cannot create alone," says Martin George. "We knew our brand and our commercial objectives. tangerine brought a product that was uniquely compelling."

Below: A crucial part of the second generation seat was to redefine the kinematic path. In its lounging 'z' position, the seat was designed to provide optimum comfort when very reclined.

Right: Details of various elements showing the coherence between soft and hard products. At the bottom is the Lumisty screen. A high-tech material opaque at eye level but transparent from the top, it provides visibility for the crew when serving but privacy for adjacent passengers who are unable to see each other.

It is a relationship that has continued and deepened. BA's next challenge to the team came when tangerine was asked to take its ideas into the First Class cabin. Working with design agency forpeople, tangerine delivered the next generation of luxury travel for BA First.

Once again, the team were able to find extra space within the strict confines of an aircraft interior, designing a wider and more comfortable bed while still keeping 14 seats in the cabin. BA's Design Lead Peter Cooke speaks of the airline's incredible history with tangerine. "We regard them as an agency at the very pinnacle of cabin and seat design and we've had a great relationship working hand-in-hand with them."

For Matt Round, the definition of 'clever design' is "forging connections so you harmonise rather than compromise". In other words, the secret is contained within the philosophy of yin and yang.

Below: A detailed specification document created when tendering to potential suppliers for the re-design of BA's First cabin. Design can become limited through the procurement process and this ensures misunderstandings can't occur and design quality is protected.

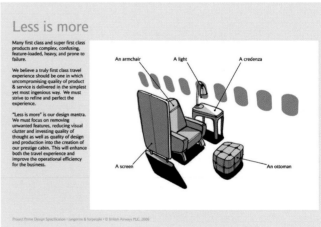

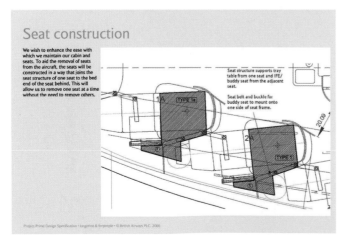

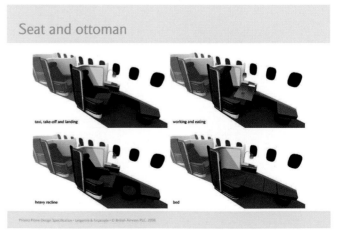

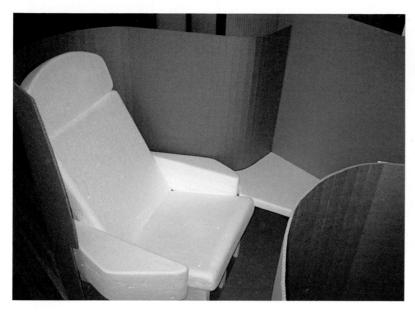

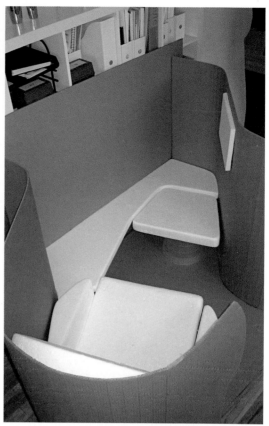

Above and right: Simple full-size card and white-foam mock-ups are highly effective at assessing the spatial benefits of the concepts.

Below: More detailed mock-ups are then frequently built, enabling evaluation by customers and for user trials.

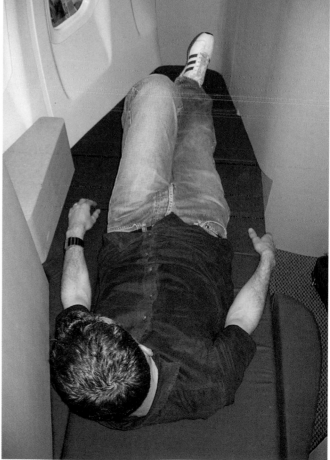

Delivering design quality in
BA First Class came from
combining the different skills
of forpeople and tangerine to
deliver a perfect result.
Understated elegance is
achieved through meticulous,
thoughtful design.

09

New technology requires
mutual understanding:
engineers to comprehend the
consumer; consumers to grasp
the engineering. Great design
releases its promise.

The day the Sky fell in

Pace | 1999

For years, the challenge of setting the video recorder was comedy shorthand for humanity's struggle with evil technology; the remote control handset with dozens of buttons and a brooding black box that conspired to embarrass you by taping the test card or, more often, nothing at all.

In the late 90s, Pace Micro Technology was making TV set-top boxes and remotes for other businesses. But Marketing Director Andrew Wallace had ambitious plans to develop the company's products and, at the same time, put an end to the jokes about VCRs and technophobes. "Product Design wasn't the thing when I joined Pace," Wallace reveals. "I held a contest to put a team of designers at the heart of company development, a contest that ended with tangerine."

Peter Phillips headed tangerine's successful pitch. "Pace changed its view of how design can change a business," he says. "They realised that instead of being something you applied at the last minute, design could be used from the start as a selling tool."

It was a massive psychological shift for a company like Pace. Rather than the primary focus on engineering and technology, they would look to make consumer-friendly products within a clear brand identity.

"Our job was to strip out complexity and cost wherever we could, and build in a design DNA," says tangerine CEO Martin Darbyshire. "They were mostly making set-top boxes for cable and satellite providers. The challenge was to create an easily recognisable design language for Pace."

Then in 1999, in the midst of this complex brand development process, something quite startling happened. It was the day the Sky fell in. A team from the satellite broadcaster BSkyB described a television system they wanted Pace to make, which for the very first time, would allow people to record, pause, rewind and replay live television and be integrated fully into the company's programme guide. "It was a clunky but extraordinary presentation," Andrew Wallace remembers. "It was one of those really rare moments when you know immediately – this is going to be brilliant."

"What they had come up with was a combination of two things – the video recorder and the set-top box," says Darbyshire. "It was the moment of conception for integrated time-shift TV."

Left: Second generation Sky+ set-top box.

Below: Hand controller designed for the set-top box manufacturer Pace. This product didn't go into production.

1992

Left: Renderings showing the related design language of the Digibox and the Sky+ box. The Digibox operated just as a set-top whereas for the first time the Sky+ box combined that with a personal video recorder. The design language reflects the television sets of that era rather than today's flat screens.

1999

Left: Showing the design language relating the Mini-box, the Digibox and the Sky+ box. The design language reflects the transition from CTR and the emergence of flat screen TV technology and DVD players.

Left: Sky Mini-box.

After an 18-month gestation, Europe's first ever Personal Video Recorder (PVR) would be born, christened Sky+. While Pace's engineers concentrated on getting the digital system right, tangerine's job was to create a box and controls that consumers could understand.

"We take it for granted now, but it was an amazing idea then that you could pause live TV," says Mike Woods. "It's difficult to imagine how revolutionary this was at the time." Peter Phillips realised users might have trouble getting their heads around the new device. "When it happened, it was like, what – there's no tape and you record on a hard drive?" he recalls. Mike Woods saw the job as trying to humanize the technology. "We needed to look at who would be watching and how," he explains. "The whole experience had to be easy to fathom and to operate."

Every two weeks for three years, Woods travelled up to Pace's HQ near Leeds from the tangerine office in London. On the train, he found himself wrestling with a conundrum posed by the new technology – the hard drive meant it was not obvious when the Sky+ box was recording, spooling or playing.

"We could have gone for a normal dot matrix display, but that would have been too expensive," says Phillips. "Then Mike came up with an answer – a ring of spinning LED lights." It was a beautifully simple and inexpensive idea. "The ring of LEDs was developed as a way of showing someone what the thing was doing when you were using it," says Darbyshire. "If you recorded the news, you'd see the wheels spinning to say it was doing it. It was about confirming in someone's mind that the right thing was happening."

The ring of LEDs, though, was destined to be far more than a source of visual encouragement for a consumer. The company made the shape central to the Sky+ branding. "It would become the visual icon that represented this and all subsequent generations of Sky+ services," Phillips says. Wallace agrees that the LED ring was the most eye-catching aspect of the box. "Occasionally you work on products that you know will fly," he says, "so we knew this was going to be really good, we just didn't know how good."

The bosses at BSkyB believed that the combination of new technology and smart design in the Sky+ box could be a game-changer. A £20-million advertising campaign was launched, particularly trying to appeal to potential customers who might feel overwhelmed by the complexity of digital TV.

"Sky+ is a truly great product, which is why we have put it at the core of all our marketing," BSkyB's Jon Florsheim told the press. "It is so advanced and so good that we believe it will have a halo effect on the entire BSkyB brand."

Although the Sky+ box was initially a small part of the company's overall market, the people who got it loved it. Customer satisfaction was monitored by the 'churn rate' – the number of machines sent back because they were no longer wanted. "While the overall fall-out amongst Sky customers was more than 9 per cent, where Sky+ was concerned, excluding deaths and divorces, it was virtually zero," Florsheim reveals.

What tangerine had helped achieve was a low-cost product packed with extraordinary technology that looked stylish and was intuitive to use. "It was magic for Pace," Andrew Wallace says. "Pace became the biggest player in Europe and eventually biggest in the world." From 1998 to 2003, when Wallace was at the company, the share price went from 25p to £13.

Top: Detailed view of the main controls and ring of spinning LED lights, which became the hallmark of Sky+. The controls took design cues from other contemporary record/playback devices like VCRs.

Above: Second generation of Sky+ showing the key controls.

"Occasionally you work on products that you know will fly. So we knew that this was going to be really good, we just didn't know how good!"

Andrew Wallace, former Marketing Director, Pace

Below: Ring of LEDs that would provide the halo effect for BSkyB.

Above: Sky+ advertising hoarding.

For Mike Woods, now lecturing at Plymouth University, the little ring of spinning LEDs that sits on the front of the Sky+ box is one of his proudest achievements. "If you say you developed the Business Class seat, most people will shrug because they may have only flown easyJet and always turn right rather than left on a plane" he says. "But this is in every housing estate, from Land's End to John O'Groats."

The little ring of LEDs may also explain why you rarely hear the old joke about the agonies of setting the video any more.

10

In order to see, first one
must look: sometimes the
stories that drive passions and
products are not told in words.

The cutting edge of design

Wilkinson Sword | 2002

It is not often that a designer has to worry that carrying a product prototype might lead to a night in the cells. But as Mike Woods headed off for a client meeting in London, he couldn't help feeling slightly nervous at the thought of trying to explain the 18cm (7in) long blade in his bag.

The son of a Devon farmer, Woods regarded the project as a dream come true. He'd been asked to design a survival knife for Wilkinson Sword. "I grew up on a farm where people carried knives as a matter of course," the former tangerine Creative Director says. "In London, people have troubling preconceptions about them. I think of a knife as a tool to cut through string on a bale of hay."

The association with Wilkinson Sword also triggered a sense of pride and heritage – the company is associated with the finest military swords. During the Second World War, British Commandos notoriously carried the company's stiletto dagger and, after the Battle of Stalingrad in 1943, Churchill presented Stalin with a bejewelled longsword bearing the Wilkinson Sword name.

For Woods, this was no normal product and no normal customer. "They were the perfect client, really, looking to reposition themselves as a manufacturer of knives for modern sportsmen," he recalls.

Branding expert Simon May helped hone a corporate identity based on Wilkinson Sword's reputation for 'craftsmanship with precision'. "They had no experience of working with designers, but they came at the project with an open attitude, trusting tangerine to advise them on the right product and image."

tangerine needed advice, too, though. This was a product that had to survive in one of the most demanding niche markets – the world of survival itself. Buyers would be enthusiasts and collectors, who often think nothing of pitting themselves against the elements armed only with a knife.

"The key to great design is often great research – but it has to be the right kind," says Woods. "We could have spoken to the survival knife community, but my concern was that they would simply give us a list of what they thought they wanted." True innovation often comes from identifying the things people don't realise they want.

Left: A detail of the CSK 185 Dartmoor survival knife.

Above: Observation of Royal Marine survival training experts helped unlock insights.

Below: Instructions for the the original Wilkinson Sword survival knife, designed by Ray Mears.

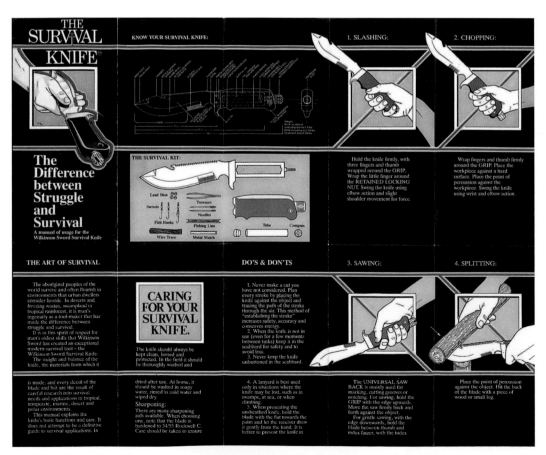

"We could have spoken to the survival knife community, but my concern was that they would simply give us a list of what they thought they wanted. True innovation often comes from identifying the things people don't realise they want."

Mike Woods

So, instead, he went to the Royal Marines. They agreed to take Woods and a small arsenal of survival knives out onto Dartmoor. His job was just to watch. "By simply observing them, I saw them do things intuitively that they didn't even realise they were doing," Woods says. This knife wasn't going to end up as part of the military kit, but the Marines knew how to handle a Wilkinson Sword blade – a carbon steel knife originally supplied by the company is still part of their equipment. They were also experts in survival.

"This one blade had to do lots of things – chop heavy stuff, split things, cut at a fine level, and one part needed to be used more like a hammer or maul," Woods says. "By watching closely how heavy knives are used, we were able to optimise the geometry and functionality of this blade."

A survival knife, according to professional bushcraft instructor Paul Kirtley, is "a product designed first and foremost to help you out of an unspecified difficult situation what or wherever that may be". For Woods and the tangerine team, the challenge was to turn all the research into a tool that would fulfil that demanding spec.

The result was an impressive steel, double-edged knife and sheath with hidden attributes. The CSK 185 (Combination Survival Knife) contained a button compass, snare wire, fishing line with weights, swivels and hooks, a scalpel blade, fire flash and even sewing needles (one for darning, one for sail-making). Other features allowed the user to collect and purify water.

Woods, though, wanted to see what his Marine friends made of it. "This is a bit Gucci," said one sceptically as he pulled it from its sheath. But despite its design good looks, the unit quickly gave the knife a thumbs-up. "It's all right, that – it works!" said one. "I like the grip on that," said another. "Nice," a third agreed. For Woods, you couldn't ask for better feedback.

Paul Kirtley tested the knife in a survival situation – heading into the wilderness with just the CSK 185 to sustain him. "I was able to do everything I needed," he says, adding how "the shape of the knife has become a classic of survival tool design".

The wider survival community loved it, too. Without any marketing, the knife sold twice as many as predicted. At the time, it retailed at £165. A decade later, and a numbered edition could fetch three times that.

Ray Sterling, who runs a survival supplies company, bought scores of the CSK 185, but now has only a few left. "I took it on a survival course myself and everyone was borrowing it," he says. "I still use mine two or three times a week for cutting and splitting – there's nothing better." It is no surprise that the knife won a number of design awards.

Unfortunately, an iconic product had come too late for the perfect client. The army had decided to put the contract to make ceremonial swords out to tender and the Wilkinson Sword factory closed. "With the widespread desirability of this knife combined with Wilkinson Sword's sad demise, it was almost inevitable that this classic knife would quickly become a collector's item," Paul Kirtley reflects.

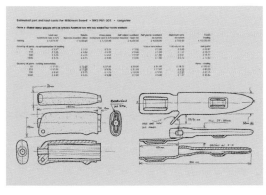

Above: Design is an investment and small companies need to know potential project costs before committing. Here simple sketches were used to get preliminary quotes from suppliers for both tooling and parts.

BY APPOINTMENT TO
H.M. QUEEN ELIZABETH II
SWORD CUTLERS
WILKINSON SWORD LTD
LONDON

BY APPOINTMENT TO
H.R.H. THE DUKE OF EDINBURGH
SWORD CUTLERS
WILKINSON SWORD LTD
LONDON

Above: The WS logo was recrafted and modernised with a design by David Baird.

Below: For the Wilkinson Sword brand, a corporate identity was created that would work in both modern and traditional contexts.

BRAND FRAMEWORK

Purpose
'craftsmanship with precision'

Promise
'every product we make is crafted with precision'

Crafted
handmade
heritage
history
tradition
unique

Precision
technology
quality
desire

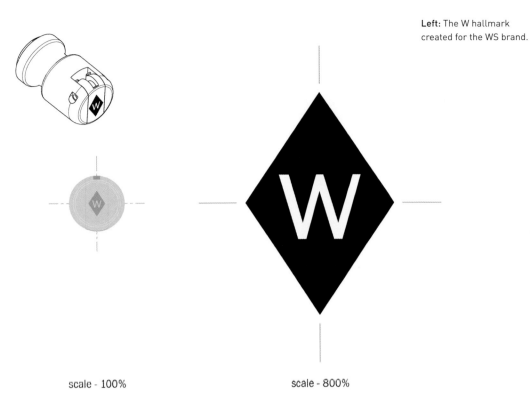

Left: The W hallmark created for the WS brand.

Below: Packaging was created to appeal to the customer who might also be a collector. It was in great contrast to that found on other hunting/survival products.

scale - 100%

scale - 800%

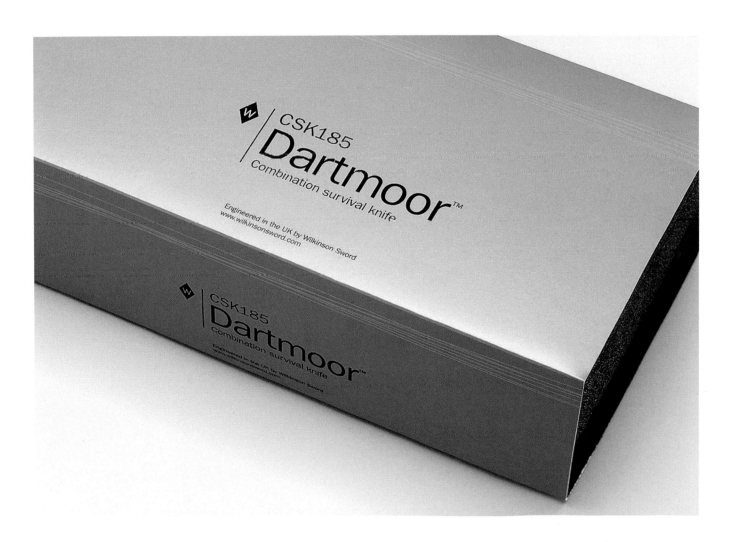

Production samples of the knife and and its reversible scabbard. The co-moulded rubber handle delivers significantly better performance than the original design. All the elements of the knife, including the double-edged blade and sheath containing compass, fishing line, snare wire, swivels, hooks and needles, have been designed to tell a story about the different dimensions of survival techniques.

11

The keys to unlocking commercial
success are often hidden within
the subconscious of the consumer.
The skill is in finding and
exploiting them.

The secrets of Europe's bedrooms

Auping | 2004

When it comes to the bedroom, are you an adventurer? Or a cosy nester? Do you like your mattress hard and supportive? Or soft and welcoming? The answer to such questions may well depend on where you live. How we go to sleep is shaped by the culture that surrounds us, and so designing a successful bed for an international market means understanding the subtle local variations in the way people sleep.

"We needed help to make sure we weren't thinking too Dutch," says Thom Verheggen, then Project Manager at the Netherlands-based bed manufacturer Auping. The company had ambitions to create Europe's 'ultimate bed' but knew that being 'famous in Holland' was not enough.

"I'd seen what tangerine had done designing the adjustable bed for British Airways' Club World cabins and thought they would be the right people to help Auping take its brand forward," says Mirjam van Coillie, the company's Design Director at the time. And there was seemingly much to do. Matt Round, tangerine's Creative Director, cast his eye over Auping's bestsellers. "To most of Europe," he says, "they looked like hospital beds."

In the Netherlands, being able to adjust your bed is considered quite normal, but getting other countries to buy into the Auping slumber experience was not going to be an easy task. So tangerine devised an intensive six-day programme, investigating the habits and foibles of Europe's bedrooms. "Matt did some research and what people wanted came to life," says Verheggen. Consumers in different parts of Europe were asked what rest and relaxation meant to them. "We gained a profound insight into what users expect and it really made us think."

"We learned that people in southern Europe generally like their beds hard," says van Coillie. "It's hot, so they want to sleep on top. In colder climates up north, they go for softer beds that surround them more and keep them warm." The Germans tended to favour functional and minimal beds. The Danes preferred an intimate, relaxing environment. National preferences emerged, but so did common European values.

One piece of feedback proved inspirational for Matt Round. "A Swedish woman told us how she would look at lovely clouds and think how nice it would be to be bouncing up and down on them." From that fragment of consumer intelligence, the idea for a 'floating mattress' was born. The engineers in the Auping factory worked with tangerine to produce a mattress with a changing profile, supporting the body more where it needs it – in the torso and hips, which are considerably heavier than the legs.

"What's really interesting is when you encourage people to stop talking about the beds and start talking about the experience – the sensations," says Round. "What the Swedish lady was really thinking about was the way a bed touches her skin, showing how important the first contact is."

Auping's association with adjustability was echoed in a product designed to adapt to different bedroom behaviours. "The point was to give people freedom to move things around so that the space felt comfortable for them," says Round. "We wanted them to be able to personalise the bedroom to suit their style."

Sleep scientists, lighting specialists and ergonomists all had an input in creating the ultimate bed for different consumer groups. Three distinct types were identified – 'cosy nesters', 'adventurers' and 'good taste', with an accessory strategy devised for each. "Matt has great eyes and ears – he is a very good observer and listener," Verheggen says. "We got to see our potential customers in flesh and blood."

Unfortunately, the Europe-wide financial crisis in 2007 took the spring out of the luxury bedding market and Auping put plans for the ultimate bed on hold. But elements of the design work and innovations have been used in other beds in the Auping range and, whatever else, peeking into bedrooms resulted in a victory for improved European understanding.

> "What's really interesting is when you encourage people to stop talking about the beds and start talking about the experience – the sensations."
> **Matt Round**

Left: Recorded research interviews revealed consumers' key insights and unmet needs, directing design development.

Below: Stimulus boards encouraging interviewees to discuss their experiences, feelings and aspirations.

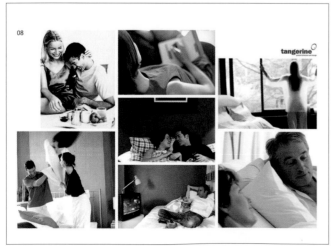

Right and below: Early sketches exploring alternative concept directions.

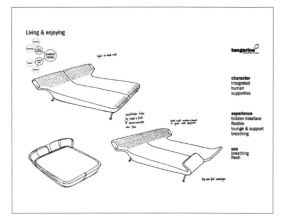

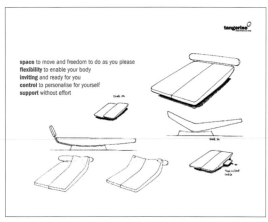

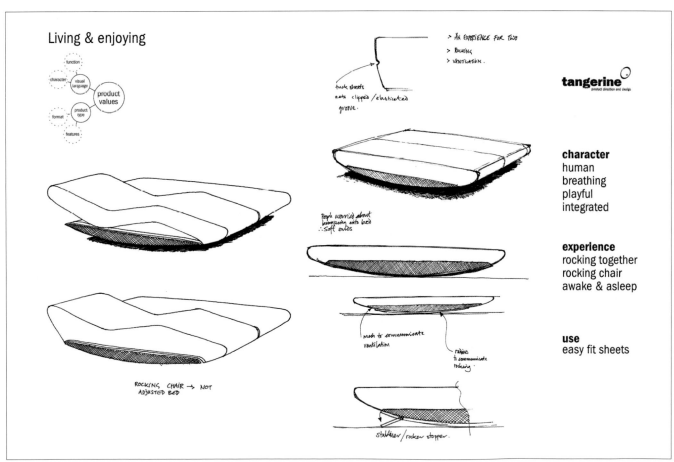

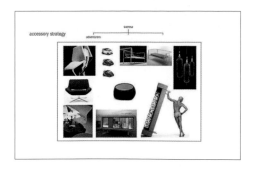

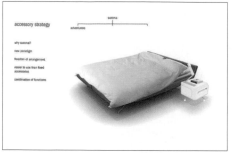

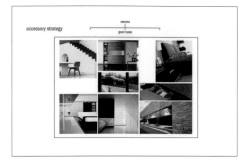

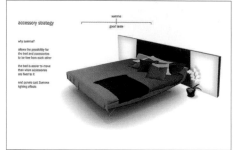

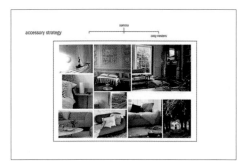

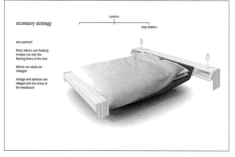

Above: Directional moodboards and designs taken from the accessory strategy aligning beds with added features with different consumer groups.

"We gained a profound insight into what users expect and it really made us think."

Thom Verheggen, former Project Manager, Auping

Previous: Prototype development at Auping's upholstery factory in Eindhoven and at the frame building plant in Deventer.

12

Design spirit is distilled from past and future, familiar and unique. Skilfully blended, its flavour is distinctive, consistent and instantly recognisable.

Feeling at home in Korea

Samsung | 1998–2010

The corporate-branded apartment is a peculiarly South Korean phenomenon. In the last few decades, thousands upon thousands of largely unremarkable rectangular residential blocks have been constructed by the country's giant business conglomerates. Fifty years ago only 1 per cent of the population lived in such a home, but the economic transformation of South Korea has been such that today 60 per cent of people occupy an apartment block, often stamped with a company name and unit number.

"In 2005, when Samsung C&T came to us, there was little to differentiate their homes from those of their competitors, Hyundai or GS," says tangerine President Don Tae Lee. "The skyline of Seoul was dominated by row upon row of characterless company housing." Don and the tangerine office had come recommended, having already completed a number of successful projects for Samsung Electronics, Korea's number one brand.

Samsung C&T is the construction arm of the huge Samsung Corporation, with an international reputation for extraordinary engineering: they built the celebrated Petronas Towers in Malaysia and the tallest building in the world, the Burj Khalifa in Dubai. Their domestic architecture, however, was much less glamorous. "Our company wasn't really thinking about the buyers of these apartments," admits Seung Min Kim, Samsung C&T's former Design Division Director. "Korean workers required housing and we just provided it." All that was about to change, however.

"At the end of the 90s I realised we needed to have a design mission in what we were doing with our apartments," Seung says. "We needed to be different." He developed a concept that eventually took shape with the help of tangerine.

"I was introduced to C&T through the work we had done with Samsung's electronics division," Don explains. He was given the title Design Master and his own office at C&T. "I soon found myself working one or two days a week inside their building, devising a design strategy and philosophy for them. Seung had called the project Raemian, a Korean word associated with future beauty and well-being."

tangerine Creative Director Matt Round and Project Director Young Choo were commissioned to help Don breathe life into the design spirit of

Raemian. "We organised workshops with the Samsung C&T executives and discussed, for example, how to inject more Korean-ness into the design," Round reveals. "The lines found under the rooftop of traditional Korean buildings were incorporated into contemporary styling. The features of traditional Korean pottery, the high glaze finish and vivid colours, were reflected in the apartments' decor."

"We also nailed down the core values of the Samsung brand and pulled out the three most important aspects – culture, nature and foresight," adds Young. "From those we developed a 'future heritage' design philosophy or spirit encompassing the key strategies of 'modern legacy', 'sensual richness' and 'human tech'."

The design spirit was based on the principle that something contemporary should also create a legacy, that it would be worth keeping because it had a lasting value. Modern Korea, tangerine believed, should connect the past with the present and relevance with difference. "Raemian apartments were aimed at the luxury market," says Young. "We looked at areas that needed to be improved so people felt it was worth what they were paying." The philosophy was applied to everything from light switches and power points to the landscaping and the colour of the carpets. "By using high contrast colours, we made the apartments feel fresher and brighter – it gave them more richness," Round says. "When we started, everything – walls, ceilings, cupboards, etc. – had a sort of plastic lino over everything."

As the design spirit was taking shape, Seung and his Korean colleagues went to London, where Young showed them what luxury apartments looked like in the UK capital. "It was really important that the in-house team could go to London," Seung says. "It gave them global awareness, confidence and pride."

By no means everything tangerine suggested found its way into the apartment in exactly the form they had envisaged, but the attention to detail quickly marked out the Raemian homes. "Within a year they had started to win design awards and soon became the sought-after brand," Seung remembers. "We were building more than ten thousand apartments each year and it wasn't very long before Raemian was number one."

It has remained at number one ever since with "Raemian" having almost become Korean shorthand for chic sophistication. There is even a gallery dedicated to the Raemian style. tangerine's input into the project continued for more than six years, with Don maintaining his office at C&T Headquarters. "Sometimes when I look across Seoul at night I am surprised by how dominant they appear," he says, "but I am very proud."

"Other companies have now set up design teams and design divisions," says Seung. "Some teams from overseas have even sent engineers to copy everything, but I am not offended – Raemian is the thing of which I am most proud. It is wonderful."

"Within a year they had started to win design awards and soon became the sought-after brand. We were building more than ten thousand apartments each year and it wasn't very long before Raemian was number one."
Seung Min Kim, former Design Division Director, Samsung C&T

Design Spirit

Human tech
Responsive
Uncomplicated
Usable
Refined
Technically capable

Future Heritage

Modern legacy
Modern interpretations of traditional forms
Respectful of history
Contemporary in Expression

Sensual richness
Genuine
Multi-textural
Polysensorial
Protection & warmth

RAEMIAN

Modern Legacy

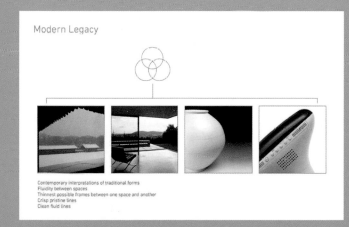

Contemporary interpretations of traditional forms
Fluidity between spaces
Thinnest possible frames between one space and another
Crisp pristine lines
Clean fluid lines

Sensual Richness

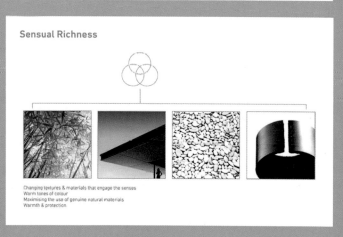

Changing textures & materials that engage the senses
Warm tones of colour
Maximising the use of genuine natural materials
Warmth & protection

Top: Raemian design spirit looking at three different themes: 'modern legacy', 'sensual richness' and 'human tech'. This spirit leads designers to create a visual language that will be used consistently across the Raemian apartment complex, from interiors to outdoor space.

Above and right: Moodboards that explore the imagery for each design theme, helping designers interpret the design spirit.

Human Tech

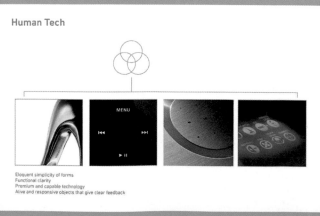

Eloquent simplicity of forms
Functional clarity
Premium and capable technology
Alive and responsive objects that give clear feedback

Left: Built-in kitchen system showing appliances designed in accordance with the design spirit.

Right: Hand-drawn sketch showing the construction of the gas burners on the hob.

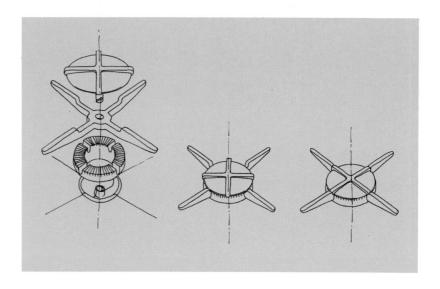

Below: Final design of the gas hob. Each individual burner is visually linked to a control dial by a blue LED light, making use of the hob more intuitive.

Above: Interior of the entrance and hall of a Raemian block. Traditional Korean patterns are used in a modern context.

Right: A bathroom informed by Korean cultural trends. A small foot bath sits below the hand basin with both integrated into the bath area to create a complete unit.

Left: Raemian complex showing the street furniture, lighting and landscape design.

Below left, clockwise: Entrance, drain cover, signage, communal outdoor furniture.

Below: Basement parking signage using natural materials and new graphics to help orientation and give a calm and pleasing ambiance.

13

Authenticity is a vital strand
of successful business DNA.
One must find it, map it and
exploit it to build a great brand.

The ABC of a beautiful Korean brand

AMOREPACIFIC | 2006

When two Koreans meet, there is a ceremony of greeting and introduction, a strict etiquette shaped over centuries. It is a respectful ritual that allows each to look the other in the eye to judge status and intent. When Korean companies introduce themselves to potential customers, they want their corporate character and philosophy to shine through. Without a word being spoken, the company brand must respectfully communicate the essence of the organisation.

For 60 years, AMOREPACIFIC had been a familiar presence in the beauty departments of the top Seoul department stores. But with the new millennium, the company felt it was time to introduce itself to the wider world, to consumers across Asia as well as Europe and the United States. "We really wanted to reach out to the global market," says AMOREPACIFIC's former Senior Manager Tae-Kyung Lee. "But it is hard for a Korean company to do that." The company realised it needed help with the introductions and knocked on the door of tangerine's recently opened office in the South Korean capital.

The door was opened by Don Tae Lee, tangerine's President and, coincidentally, an old college friend of Tae-Kyung. "What they wanted was to be more of a global brand and also to change the perception of AMOREPACIFIC in their domestic market," Don recalls. "At the time, they were not perceived as premium and luxury in the same way as the top European brands."

With teams working in both Seoul and London, tangerine were the perfect design partners for a client wanting to appeal to Asian and Western consumers without betraying their Korean roots.

The immediate challenge was to devise a corporate logo for AMOREPACIFIC, a new calling card for this ambitious company. "What we wanted was something that related specifically to AMOREPACIFIC and our heritage," Tae-Kyung explains. "We had a great brand, but we needed a motif to soften our image and express our corporate identity."

tangerine's London team asked graphic designer David Baird to help them with the project. Baird had designed tangerine's own corporate marque and came with a reputation for meticulous and studious work.

Right: Six guiding design themes were established through research and intense discussion with AMOREPACIFIC. Key words and imagery were developed, summarising and expressing their essence.

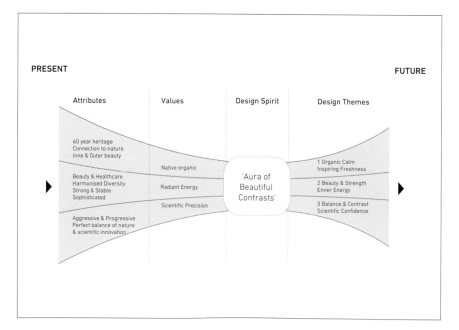

LOCAL BRANDS

Names, symbols &
associations that can be
Developed locally
Tailored to a local market
Selected without the
constraints of a global brand

Reduced risk from
'buy local' sentiments

Can be controlled centrally
but implemented locally

KOREA   ASIA   WORLD

GLOBAL BRANDS

Scale economies in the
development of
Advertising
Packaging
Point of sale
Marcoms

Exploitation of
Media
Exposure to customers
who travel

Associations
of a global presence

PRESENT   FUTURE

Attributes   Values   Design Spirit   Design Themes

60 year heritage
Connection to nature
Inne & Outer beauty

Native organic

'Aura of
Beautiful
Contrasts'

1 Organic Calm
Inspiring Freshness

Beauty & Healthcare
Harmonised Diversity
Strong & Stable
Sophisticated

Radiant Energy

2 Beauty & Strength
Enner Energy

Aggressive & Progressive
Perfect balance of nature
& scientific innovation

Scientific Precision

3 Balance & Contrast
Scientific Confidence

Top left: This diagram was created to help AMOREPACIFIC to understand the key strategic issues behind being either a local or a global brand.

Left: Early work focused on defining and articulating the unique attributes and core values of the business. This was used to create a design spirit to give coherence across all brand touch-points.

Native origins

Natural Calm
Native organics

Undulating surfaces
Irregularity
Rough & smooth
Shimmering surfaces
Natural beauty
Fluid & flowing
Organic forms

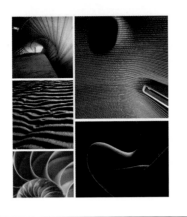

Inspiring freshness
Native organics

Lightness
Brightness
Small detailing
Youthfulness
Clean
Revealing
Translucence

Radiant energy

Beauty & strength
Radiant energy

Control
Elegance
Taught
Cocoon
Protection

Inner Energy
Radiant energy

Glow from within
Breathing
Dynamic forms
Confidence
Vision
Alive
Renewal

Scientific precision

Balance & Contrast
Scientific precision

Science & Nature
Rough & smooth
Strength & sensitivity
Controlled fluidity
The art of science

Scientific Confidence
Scientific precision

Ice cool
Controlled
Precision
Clear & concise
Evidence
Measured & considered

"My friends nickname me the 'designosaur', as I work just with a pen and a sketch pad," he says. "On this project after the initial meetings with the client in Seoul, I remember doing a lot of writing around the page; in this case words like green tea, Korea and camellia and then slowly formulating ideas on paper."

The words reflected AMOREPACIFIC's origins, starting out as local traders in the medicinal and cosmetic properties of camellia flowers and green tea. As the motif began to take shape, symbols of that heritage blossomed in Baird's notebooks – the outlines of tea leaves, camellia blossom and hearts, gathered in a circle to evoke global consciousness. "I also did days of work on how you could use elements of it," he says, "cropping it or not having it centred, so it could be used in all different scenarios."

"The motif was very fresh and quite unlike anything seen in Korea before," says Tae-Kyung. "It really related to AMOREPACIFIC and the elements could be taken apart and applied in other circumstances, so it was very flexible." The motif in its various forms found its way onto carrier bags, company trucks, stationery and across corporate branding. A pink version was even sported by the chief executive to support breast cancer research.

The response to the motif was so positive that AMOREPACIFIC asked tangerine to help devise a design philosophy for the expanding corporation. "We started with brand positioning work," tangerine Creative Director Matt Round remembers. "Luxury Western brands tend to base their appeal on the romance and glamour of big cities like Paris or New York. Seoul at that time simply didn't have that aura." Instead, Round and the tangerine team worked on writing a design spirit story based on AMOREPACIFIC's core values. "It was about their heritage, their connection to nature, their medical wisdom and their determination to improve people's well-being," says Round. "The challenge then was to communicate that in a credible way that would work in the east and the west."

Part of that challenge was to update the corporation's word marque – AMOREPACIFIC used the letters ABC in its branding, originally standing for All Best Cosmetics. "We all agreed it was a bit old-fashioned," Round says. "After a great many meetings in London and Seoul we constructed two new phrases: 'Asian Beauty Creator' to communicate the promise of the brand and 'Aura of Beautiful Contrasts', which guided the look and feel of every touch point."

"It was a close working relationship with tangerine, who always pulled out issues and also created a fine concept," Tae-Kyung remembers fondly. "I had excellent communication with Don in Seoul and the London office. What is so great is that tangerine's co-existence can mix Korean and European culture and bring in very fresh new ideas."

Aspects of the new design philosophy were taken up. "Asian Beauty Creator helped us reach out to the Asian market," Tae-Kyung reveals, "but the broader idea of a design spirit was hard for some to understand and the chief executive said we should wait and maybe use it in the future."

AMOREPACIFIC's caution perhaps reflects the significance and respect Koreans afford to ancient traditions of greeting and introduction.

"We had a great brand but we needed a motif to soften our image and express our corporate identity."
Tae-Kung Lee, Senior Manager, AMOREPACIFIC

Top: The original AMOREPACIFIC ABC logo, standing for 'All Best Cosmetics'.

Above: The redesigned ABC logo is more contemporary, confident and friendly. The letters now stand for 'Asian Beauty Creator', reflecting the design spirit.

"It was about their heritage, their connection to nature, their medical wisdom and their determination to improve people's well-being. The challenge then was to communicate that in a credible way that would work in the east and the west."
Matt Round

Right and below: The design spirit of AMOREPACIFIC, as well as key product ingredients like camellia blossom and essence of green tea, defined elements of the graphic motif, with hearts representing a love of heritage.

Harmony with inner & outer beauty

Maternal patriotism

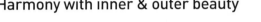

Camellia seeds

Green tea leaves

Left: Corporate identity
manual created to show how
the decorative motif is used
across all applications and
brand touch-points, from
stationery to signage and
architecture to vehicles.
AMOREPACIFIC word
marque designed by Landor
Associates.

Above: The final graphic motif.

14

Great designers teach a language that is understood across the world. Helping companies adapt their culture so they speak many dialects opens up global opportunity.

The code for international dialling

Huawei | 2007–2011

When tangerine's Creative Director Matt Round first arrived at Huawei's global HQ in 2007, he was blown away. "It was more like a city than a factory," he recalls. "The main avenue feels like you are on London's Oxford Street on a Saturday afternoon."

Founded just two decades earlier by ex-military technologist Ren Zhengfie with an investment of around $5000, Huawei is now the largest telecommunications equipment maker in the world with annual sales worth over $20 billion. Even by Chinese standards, its growth has been remarkable

Round had been invited to the vast corporate headquarters in Shenzhen to discuss how tangerine might help this ambitious Chinese company achieve global penetration. "They were looking for anywhere to sell," he remembers. "We were telling them you have to get into the cultures of the market if you want to sell. You need to know what makes your customers tick."

tangerine had originally been selected to help Huawei break into Europe. "We needed a European market product, so I tried to find the right agency," Huawei director Bin Xie says. "We didn't want an agency that just brings their familiar ways to us, we wanted them to understand our company, our products and what makes us special."

It was, though, a two-way process. Just as tangerine needed to understand the culture of Huawei, so Huawei needed to understand the culture of the Western consumer. Alongside Matt Round at those early meetings in Shenzhen was Project Manager and Senior Designer Weiwei He, a Chinese national who had also studied in London. "Weiwei knows how Chinese people think," Bin Xie says. "Weiwei has an open mind, but her position was important as a bridge between two cultures." There were times Weiwei found herself having to mediate as the business relationship developed. "Sometimes I had to say to the guys at tangerine that I understand what you are saying, but I also understand the client side," Weiwei recalls.

For Round, the approach to design at Huawei needed an urgent overhaul. "Designers were literally being given a week or two to design a

Left: Touchscreen slider phone with full QWERTY hard key keyboard.

HUAWEI C7100
CDMA 1X 数字移动电话机

手写键盘双输入　　USB即插即用高速Modem　　WAP2.0高速上网　　超强FM

简约气质，与生俱来。华为C7100，一如不事张扬的您，简约中透露不凡。它特有2.4寸QVGA绚丽大屏，助您洞悉先机，更兼备手写、键盘双输入功能，处理烦琐事务亦都得心应手。C7100与您搭档，彰显时尚商务新风范。

www.huawei.com

HUAWEI

Left: The C7100 was China's best-selling mid-tier handset in 2008.

cell phone – sometimes without even time to think and sketch," he says. "There was a sense of take something, strap some shapes on it and then see what happens." Bin Xie was impressed with the way the team from tangerine attempted subtly to adjust the design philosophy of the company. "From the first project, they were quite smart," he says. "They built a design language, and it was a balanced not an extreme solution."

Round and his colleagues introduced the Huawei executives to the importance of consumer trend analysis with data from around the world on what was happening in different markets. The aim was to impress upon them the value of a structured and strategic approach to design. "We were asked to educate their in-house team and broaden their horizons," Round explains. "I think we helped departments appreciate what good design could do for them strategically, and that meant the designers could buy themselves more time and do something better."

"Matt may be the Creative Director of tangerine," says Bin Xie, "but he's very kind to the junior designers and shares everything in a friendly way. We needed help and I like to have open talks. The mobile phone business is happening so fast and there is such a lot at stake; we need to manage the risk."

One tangible product of this new design thinking was the development of the C7100 mobile phone, designed by Weiwei. It was aimed at the Chinese market, and more than a third of a million were sold in the three months after its launch in 2008. But even more important, perhaps, was the quiet revolution tangerine had initiated as to how Huawei's products should look and feel. "They are now much simpler; they have straight lines, fewer components and have got rid of all the nonsense details," Weiwei explains. She believes tangerine has helped Huawei speak a design language that can be understood globally. "I see myself in-between China and Britain. I appreciate the simple aesthetic design that is so popular in Europe, but I also know why people in China want some more complicated shapes. So my designs are never completely European, nor entirely Chinese."

From sometimes being a last-minute addition, design has become central to Huawei's international strategy. The company now has one of the largest in-house design teams in the world with design centres in the UK, Japan and the United States as well as China. "We learned so much from tangerine," Bin Xie says.

> "You have to get into the cultures of the market if you want to sell. You need to know what makes your customers tick."
>
> Matt Round

Right: Design DNA extract, developing and guiding a coherent design language across Huawei's network terminal products.

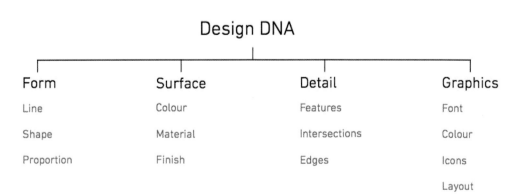

Design DNA

Form	Surface	Detail	Graphics
Line	Colour	Features	Font
Shape	Material	Intersections	Colour
Proportion	Finish	Edges	Icons
			Layout

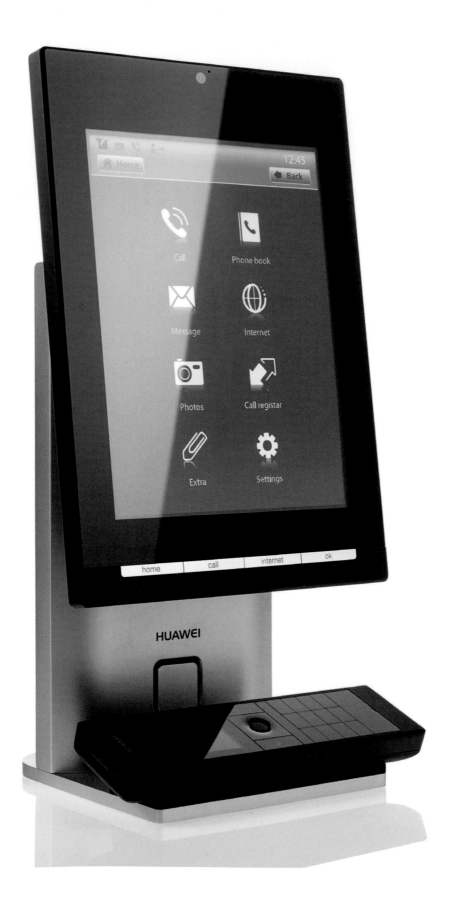

Huawei network terminals
2007:
Left: Media centre.

Right top and right centre:
Digital picture frame.

Right bottom: Modem.

Clockwise: Image boards mapping:
1) creative direction for handsets;
2) exploration of existing market segmentation;
3) scenario planning and visualisation;
4) extract from tangerine's strategic design consultancy report, which helped Huawei's Design and R&D departments have a strong voice within the business. This in turn led to more effective use of design and greater European market penetration.

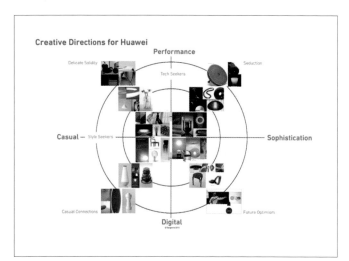

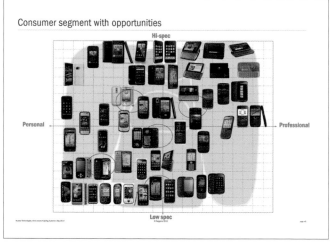

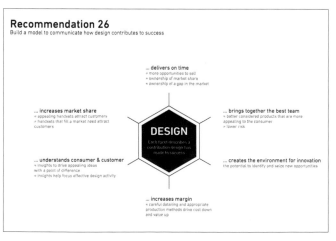

Blend Angle

GUI

The angled visual language of the GUI is harmonious with the physical form of the angled screen.

Time, date and other important functions are static.

Angled panel presents contacts with the main contact details in focus.

Other contacts in the list are slightly out of focus the further away they are.

Alphanumeric keypad is placed on an angle panel, overlayed onto the main menu. Quick access back to the main menu is directly beneath the keypad.

Pictogram apps

Menu

Instant Message

Contacts

Making Phone Call

Alll icons are placed onto angled panels with the furthieset out icons are fading out, becoming darker.

Above and right: Complete design of handset experience including UI (user interface) structure, GUI (graphic user interface) and physical product design.

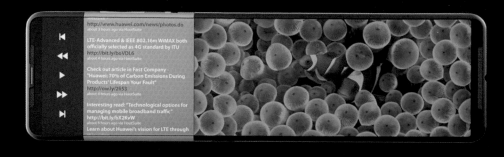

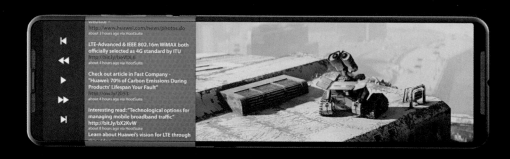

Left and below: Future tablet designed in 2009 around emerging communication behaviours of the youth market at the time.

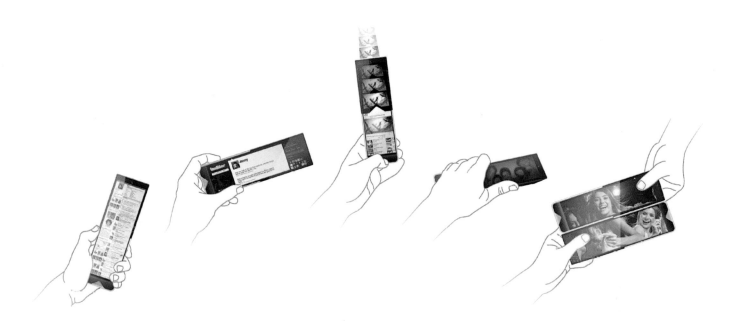

15

As an acquaintance, design may improve a business. As a close friend, design will transform it.

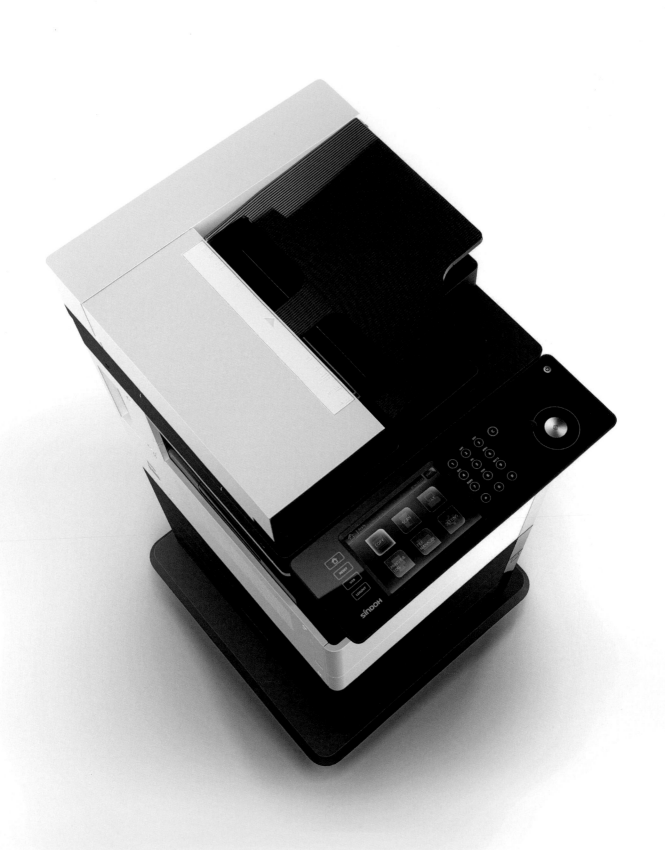

Unmistakable difference

Sindoh | 2009

Creating successful global brands and products requires designers and businesses to step across deep cultural divides – to embrace the philosophies and values of companies and markets very different from home.

When Woo Sang-ki established the Korean copier company Sindoh in 1960, he did so within the traditions of business in his country, creating a paternalistic organisation underpinned by the spirit of love for country, work and people. Sindoh's corporate declaration of love would have sounded decidedly odd in some of their Western competitors' boardrooms in the early 60s. Half a century later and the design team at tangerine found itself challenged to navigate a path between two distinct cultural philosophies while remaining true to the principles of both.

In its early years, Sindoh quickly established itself as Korea's market leader in the production of photocopiers and went on to enjoy international success making office equipment for other companies to market. However, in the mid-2000s when its engineers came up with an ingenious way of allowing A4 copiers to produce A3 copies, the CEO Dr Woo Suk-Hyung realised that they could become serious players under their own name.

"Sindoh was ready to reach out to the global market," Dr Woo says. "But we needed our own design identity and so we started to research design agencies around the world." They alighted upon tangerine with its strong connections to Korea. Dr Woo describes CEO Martin Darbyshire as having "a unique understanding of Korean sentiment".

The conduit for developing the relationship of trust between Darbyshire and Dr Woo was Young Choo, an American-educated Korean based in tangerine's London office. "Sindoh were asking very specific questions about the Western view or the global perspective and Martin was the perfect person, as he is very patient and talks through every detail," she says.

Appointing tangerine was a leap of faith for Sindoh, which had no in-house design team and had never worked with an outside agency before. For both parties, there was a steep learning curve as they tried to understand each other's way of thinking and working. The first job was to prepare the cleverly engineered A4/A3 copiers for the global market.

Left: Final design of Sindoh's black and white multifunction printer that allows A3-sized copies to be printed from an A4-sized machine.

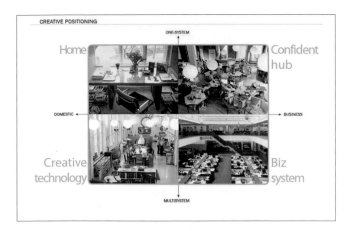

Left: Positioning map to explore the design language and brand positioning of Sindoh.

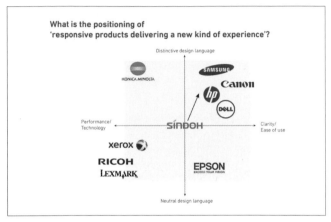

Below: Initial ideas of the new Sindoh printer.

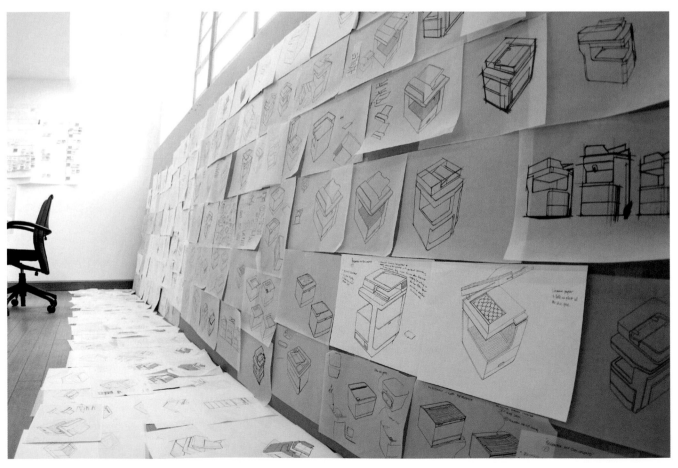

"They had no-one to help them wrap forms around the technology," says Darbyshire. "We were hired to work out what a Sindoh product should look like." Dr Woo told his workers he wanted Sindoh office machines "to be *objets*, to be sculptures".

Young Choo's role was to translate not only the words of the meetings but also the different cultures. "It was important that not only the board trusted us but also the engineers," she says. "We took them through the process step by step and were there at every stage, showing them exactly the vision for the machines."

Sindoh began to realise that the marriage of form and function envisaged by tangerine could become a key company selling point. "At that time, the printing industry was thinking more about functionality than appearance," says Dr Woo. "We believed that design identity could be one of our core competencies."

When the first of the re-designed machines hit the market in 2011, they not only scooped a series of design awards and won highly favourable press coverage, "they also sold fantastically well" according to Darbyshire.

Looking to exploit the 'halo effect' from the success of the machines, tangerine was asked to work with Sindoh on a new corporate identity. It was a process that brought the cultural differences into sharp relief and relied on the trust built up between Dr Woo and Darbyshire.

"We were asking them to think and act in ways they were not used to," Darbyshire admits. The business styles could hardly have been more different: the UK team with shirts sleeves rolled up, brainstorming around spider diagrams and endless Post-it notes; the Korean team in colour-coordinated uniforms, used to occupying set places at the table and not questioning senior management decisions.

In two days of workshops involving experts brought specially from London, including Design Connect's Michael Thomson and Will Pocknell of graphic designers DWHD, Sindoh staff were challenged to identify the strengths and weaknesses of their brand. Perhaps the most startling conclusion from the process was that 'Sindoh' wasn't really a brand at all. It was a badge. "It was surprising and a little alarming to discover that on contracts and legal documents the company retained the name 'Sindoh-Ricoh', a relic of the corporation's business-to-business identity," says Darbyshire. "The challenge for us and them was to shape a new corporate identity that announced Sindoh as a confident brand in its own right."

What emerged from the cross-cultural brainstorming was that Sindoh had strong attributes. It was seen as a thoughtful, creative and expert organisation with a distinctive character. The spirit evoked by its founder still shone through. "We wanted the powerful spirit of three that underpins the company's principles and strengths to be reflected in a new logo," Darbyshire explains. A word, strange even to English ears, had to be translated – "trimobious" – a three-sided shape made from three triangles with the intriguing properties of a Möbius strip.

"Martin clearly explains his thoughts behind design concepts and at the same time considers the position of Sindoh," says Dr Woo. "When adjustments based on our staff feedback were needed, he came up with the best solution without breaking the entire concept."

At one point, the company's very name was questioned, after consumer research suggested the 'sin' in Sindoh might be a negative in the US. Young Choo's role was to translate and examine every nuance in both languages.

> "We were asking them to think and act in ways they were not used to."
> **Martin Darbyshire**

With her help, the tangerine team was able to convince the Koreans that as the same consumers weren't worried about the 'sin' in 'sincere', Sindoh could and should remain Sindoh.

"I have come to trust Martin's philosophy," says Dr Woo. "tangerine have become like family to us."

Another potential culture clash concerned tangerine's recommendation for the company to associate itself with the word 'unmistakable'. "Annoyingly, it didn't quite translate," Darbyshire says. "In English, unmistakable means clear, distinct, definite – just right for the clear vision of this company. In Korean, it simply means 'we don't make mistakes', which doesn't work." Initially, the Sindoh executives were uncomfortable, but, encouraged by an advisor with perfect English, eventually felt confident that Sindoh's 'unmistakable' brand promise would deliver the right message to Western ears.

Navigating a path across deep cultural divides requires sensitivity and compromise. It requires sympathetic translation. Above all, though, it requires trust.

Above: Full-sized foam model of one of the chosen concepts.

Left: Full-sized final mock-up of alternative design directions.

Below: Final 3D renderings of two different products in detail.

"Martin Darbyshire has a unique understanding of Korean sentiment."

Dr Woo Suk-Hyung, CEO, Sindoh

Top to bottom: Sindoh's new range of printers that share the same design DNA.

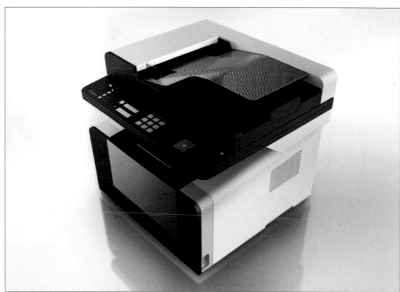

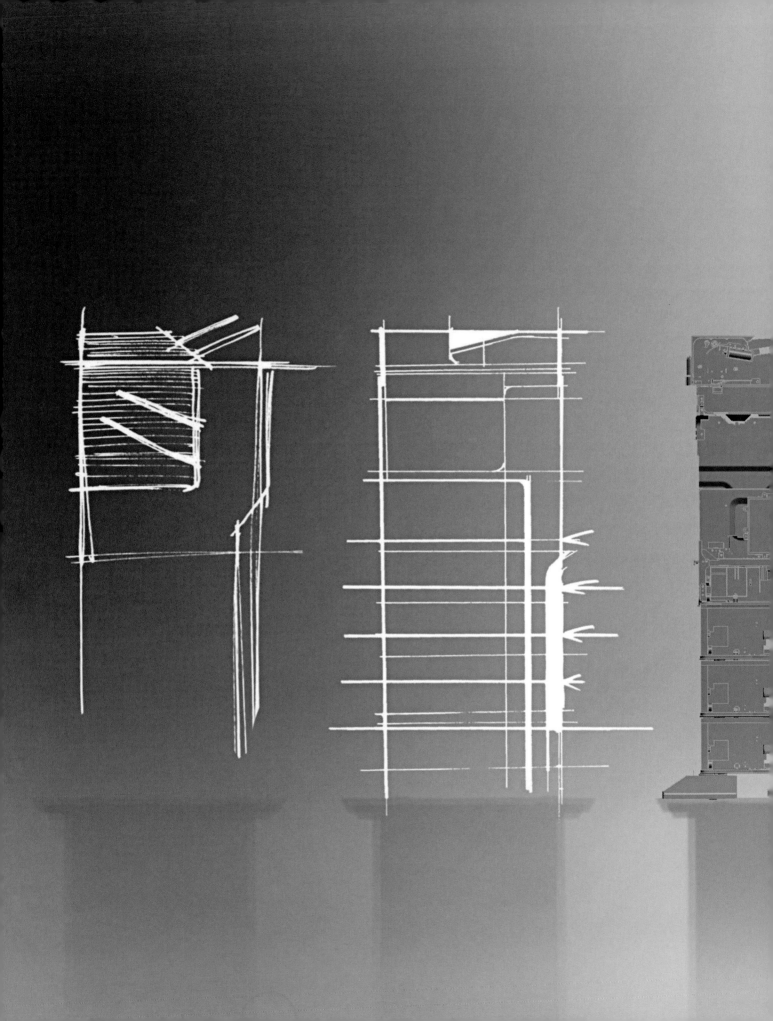

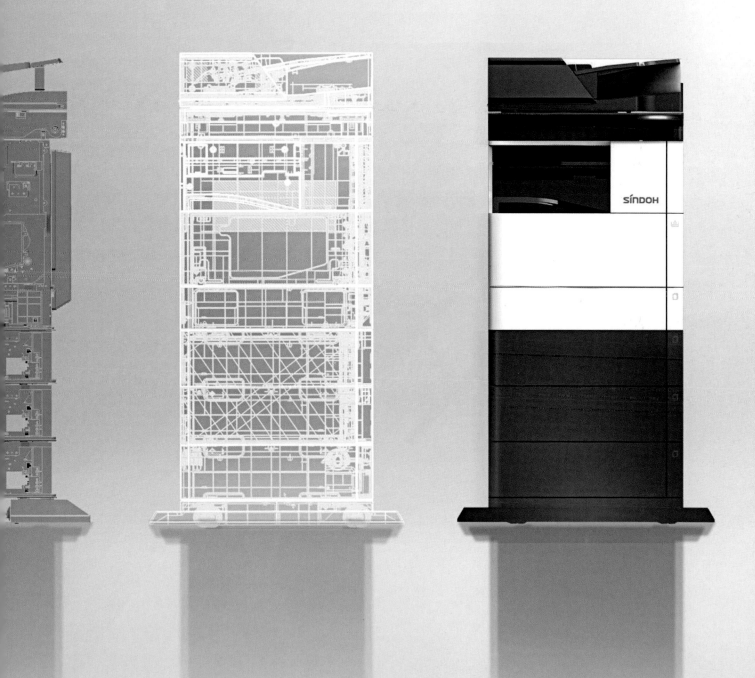

A design progression; from rough sketch through to engineering drawing and render of the final product.

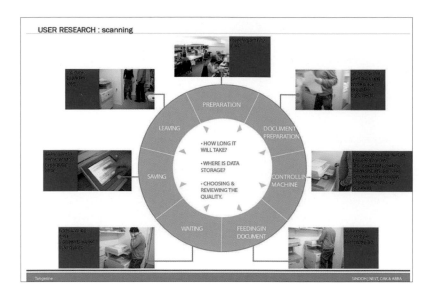

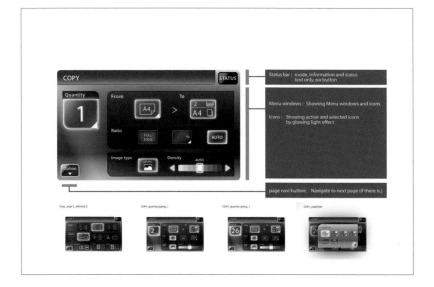

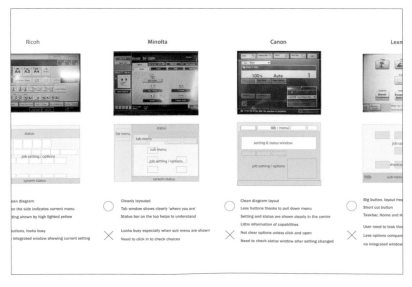

Left: Research and analysis of user behaviour.

Right: New printer with the distinctive GUI (graphic user interface) created to be aligned with the product design language.

Left: Initial stage of developing the GUI of the multifunction printer.

Right: Image showing how design has touched and influenced every aspect of Sindoh's brand and product experience.

Above: Sindoh's second generation multifunction printer.

Left: New GUI for Sindoh's high speed printer.

Top right: Sindoh's previous logo.

Clockwise:
Sindoh's new word marque and Tri-Mobius logo.

A map showing how Sindoh's new logo stands-out among the other global brands.

Brand workshop held at Sindoh's headquarters in Seoul.

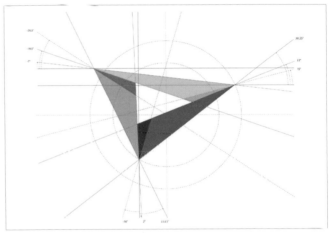

16

Technology in the wrong
clothes pushes people away.
Technology well dressed draws
cultures together.

Creating café culture

Cisco and the United Nations | 2009

The tradition of the café and the conversation stretches back hundreds of years. In early eighteenth-century England, and London in particular, there were thousands of coffee houses where people gathered on neutral territory, in a relaxed environment, to talk and to argue and to plot and to share stories. The café was the Facebook of its age.

The Dialogue Café project, supported by the United Nations Alliance of Civilization and technology giant Cisco, wanted to create a 21st-century café culture on a global scale, using the latest video conferencing equipment to enable face-to-face conversations between diverse groups from all over the world.

The very name 'Dialogue Café', though, contained the project's dilemma: it was one thing to construct the technology that allowed the dialogue, quite another to create the relaxed and welcoming world of the traditional café. "Ugly doesn't exist as a concept for engineers," says Sara Piteira, Dialogue Café Executive Director. "If something works, then it doesn't matter to them what it looks like or whether there are cables everywhere."

But in trying to create an atmosphere where young people in different cities, from different cultures, on different continents can connect in the intimate way they might around a café table, the look and feel of the technology is paramount. "It was the most challenging part of the project because engineers and designers speak different languages," Piteira says. "It involved long afternoons of intense discussion and, I admit, the Dialogue Café team came to the process knowing what they needed but with absolutely no idea how to achieve it."

The challenge was to take state-of-the-art teleconferencing technology from the austere atmosphere of a corporate boardroom into the laid-back vibe of a small café. The man who thought he knew the way was Clive Grinyer, Director of Customer Experience at Cisco and a founding member of tangerine. "Cisco had big 'TelePresence' video suites in corporations across the world so you could connect offices," Grinyer recalls. "Dialogue Café was about overcoming prejudice across countries so kids could talk to each other, so we tested the technology to see if it might work for

Left: Dialogue Café 'TelePresence' video systems in use across the world.

Above: The original 'TelePresence' video conferencing system in its corporate environment.

that project." It didn't. "People complained it felt like they were under surveillance and the equipment was very ugly," says Grinyer. "So I told Cisco we need to design it differently and I know just the people."

Grinyer went back to his old design agency with the idea and tried to enthuse tangerine Creative Director Matt Round. "When Clive first told me, I thought the technology sounded incredibly dull," Round admits, "but after seeing the TelePresence in action I was blown away. The ultra high-definition quality was extraordinary, and after a few minutes you actually forgot there was a screen between you and the people you were talking to."

The brief from Dialogue Café contained a paradox: the experience "must be intimate and social at the same time". It had to find a balance between the privacy required for an intimate chat and the openness required for a conversation involving up to 30 people. "One of the reasons we chose tangerine is we wanted them to stretch our imagination and really show us things we hadn't thought of, help us decide what a Dialogue Café really was," Grinyer says.

One concept envisaged an American diner set-up with benches facing each other. Another saw it more as a cinema experience. A third had the feel of chairs pulled around a café table.

"What tangerine did really superbly well was to develop a set of concepts that looked at different cultural contexts," Grinyer recalls. "We did a few workshops and thrashed it out with Cisco," Round says. "The final idea was to have moveable pods you connected together; a shape and an environment that encouraged conversation but where people still had some privacy. At the same time, we weren't asking them to walk into a closed space worrying that something unpleasant might happen behind the screen."

Below: Exploration of potential formats was carried out with loose sketching and imagery. Systems considered ranged from contained and rigid to moveable and highly flexible.

"What tangerine did really superbly well was to develop a set of concepts that looked at different cultural contexts."
Clive Grinyer, former Director of Consumer Experience, Cisco

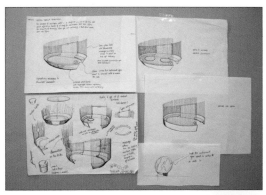

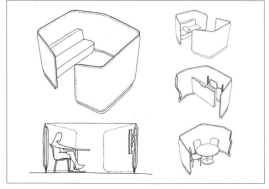

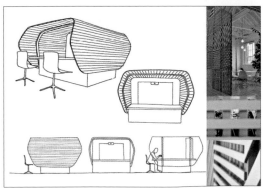

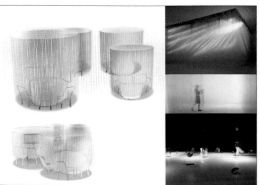

"Ugly doesn't exist as a concept for engineers. If something works, then it doesn't matter to them what it looks like or whether there are cables everywhere."

Sara Piteira, Executive Director, Dialogue Café

Right and below: Simple renderings of concepts adaptable for different meeting sizes and formats.

Above: Rudimentary card mock-ups enabling rapid assessment of the various spatial relationships, shot outside the tangerine studio in London.

Left: The first Dialogue Café booth under construction. The final product would be shipped around the world, so needed to be easily transportable.

Below: The final rendering of
the Dialogue Café booth.

"tangerine's strength was that they gave us the space to discover the right road and even when our comments made no sense they were very nice about it," says Piteira. "They didn't try to sell us a finished product but wanted to work with us to find the solution. The fact they do the mock-ups in life size makes such a difference when you are working with something like this."

tangerine went to Modus furniture to make up the pods and the clients were invited to watch the café components take shape in a Leicestershire factory. In the spring of 2010, the finished articles were shipped out to Brazil for a grand launch at a UN forum in Rio de Janeiro. Young people in Rio could talk to Lisbon in what was billed as the world's first video-conferencing network specifically designed for civil society.

"It was an incredibly exciting time and we tried all sorts of things," Piteira recalls. "We had a theatre play, music jamming in different cities and lots of talking between schools across the world." Grinyer says: "It was an installation, really – beautifully detailed, very iconic. It was friendly, it was flexible and it was highly successful – there was a real buzz about it." tangerine's work went on to win a 2010 Good Design Award.

There are now Dialogue Cafés in 12 cities around the world and, although the technology has evolved in the last few years, the spirit of 'design thinking' brought to the project by Matt Round and his team is retained. "The project made people realise that this thing called 'design' really can have an impact on the technology and really can work," says Grinyer.

"The project made people realise that this thing called 'design' really can have an impact on the technology and really can work."

Clive Grinyer, former Director of Consumer Experience, Cisco

17

Designers need to relish the challenge of operating in the most cramped conditions. The best find the small changes that add up to great success.

Spreading their wings

Korea Aerospace Industries | 2009

Modern South Korea has been described as the miracle on the River Han. In one generation the country was transformed from an impoverished rural state, devastated by war and with almost no natural resources, into one of the richest nations on the planet. Today this so-called Asian Tiger is looking to expand its export trade still further – spreading its wings, for example, from military aircraft into the civilian sector. But making that transition from no-frills combat planes to aircraft fit for wealthy Western consumers was never going to be easy. Step forward tangerine.

"The Koreans' target market was the United States," says tangerine CEO Martin Darbyshire. "They had identified a gap in the market for a four-seater light aircraft that would be cheaper than the competition. What they needed was someone to make it look creditable and meaningful in the eyes of consumers who might buy it."

Korea Aerospace Industries (KAI) knew it was flying into new territory. While the country's aviation engineering expertise was world-class, KAI Senior Researcher Taek-Jong Shin calculated that domestic understanding of what was required for a civilian cockpit was "absolutely insufficient". "We tried to find a foreign company that had experience of civil aircraft interior design even if that meant more limited communications than with a local firm," he says. "tangerine not only had great experience in this area but also had an office in Seoul which made it easy to communicate and work co-operatively." The tangerine bid easily came top in KAI's standard selection procedure.

The project still presented real challenges, though. KAI accepts they had rather left the interior design aspect of the project to the last minute. "We hadn't considered it," Taek-Jong Shin admits. "So at the end of the project there was work overload and in this difficult situation tangerine had to work flat-out for several months."

Darbyshire realised the contract was going to test all of their abilities – not only was time tight, but the space was, too. "The space in the four-seater cockpit is 2.5cm [one inch] narrower than a Smart car on the inside," he says. "Much of the instrumentation and mechanics are fixed and have to be worked round, so there really was not much room for manoeuvre."

Left: Korea Aerospace Industries' new Naraon, four-seater light aircraft.

The initial design work was done in London, with Seoul-based designer Junghyun Cho (Joey) flying to the UK with a suitcase full of regulations and rulebooks. "There are just so many things to consider – safety, fire regulations, head-clearance," Joey says. "One thing we did was work closely with an expert aircraft instructor, who helped us to understand where the instrumentation would go and how you must locate things."

In typical tangerine style, the pilot was asked to sit in exact cardboard cockpit mock-ups, offering invaluable specialist insight on the design team's ideas. "What you are trying to do is pull together all of the disparate stuff and work out what flexibility you have," Darbyshire explains. "The instrument elements are bought-in items and they get located in the right place according to where the pilot says they should go because they are hugely experienced with other aircraft. In some instances you end up able to offer options for the customer who may have particular experience of another aircraft."

Having identified the fixed points of the cockpit interior, Joey and his colleagues then set about trying to give the aircraft some style. "The shapes we could influence needed to be simple and clear," says Joey. "We are particularly proud of the flowing curve we created, the continuum from the arm-rest through the glare shield to the arm-rest on the other side. We felt it gave a sense of harmony and sophistication that our competitors didn't have."

With the 3D modelling completed in London, the project team then moved to Korea. "Even though we had presented them with an impractical plan, tangerine showed remarkable enthusiasm," jokes KAI's Taek-Jong Shin. "They had solved many of the problems because of the professional contacts they had and their understanding of interior design in the civilian market."

Overseeing the Korean end of the project was tangerine President Don Tae Lee. "I sent the team to work directly with KAI at their production centre in the far south of the country," he explains. "With such a short time-scale, it was the only way we could keep this aircraft on schedule."

The deadline was met with the client praising the "high-quality designers" who had made it happen. "We weren't able to incorporate all of tangerine's ideas," Taek-Jong Shin accepts, "but the final product is highly competitive in a market that is very hard to break."

Named 'Naraon' or 'Perfect Flight' and with a price tag of $575,000, Korea's first ever commercial light aircraft went into mass-production in 2014. It may well be remembered as a project demonstrating the determination and ambition behind the continuing miracle on the River Han – and the ability of a British design firm to rise to the challenge.

Right: Details of the final interior design of the Naraon aircraft.

"We weren't able to incorporate all of tangerine's ideas, but the final product is highly competitive in a market that is very hard to break."
Taek-Jong Shin, Senior Researcher, KAI

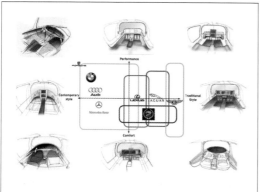

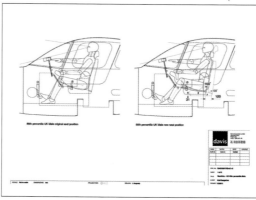

Above: Naraon light aircraft.

Far left: Initial sketches and positioning of the design language relative to key car brands, as a means of exploring different design expressions.

Left: The first step in understanding the ergonomics of the proposed interior space is to conduct anthropometric assessment from the 5th to 95th percentile.

Below left: Testing in the initial cardboard mock-up of the cockpit interior.

Right: 3D modelling showing
the view from the rear seats.

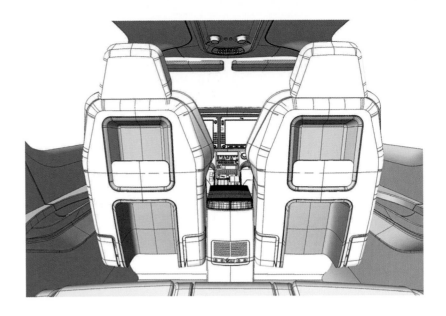

Below: Cardboard mock-up
of cockpit interior.

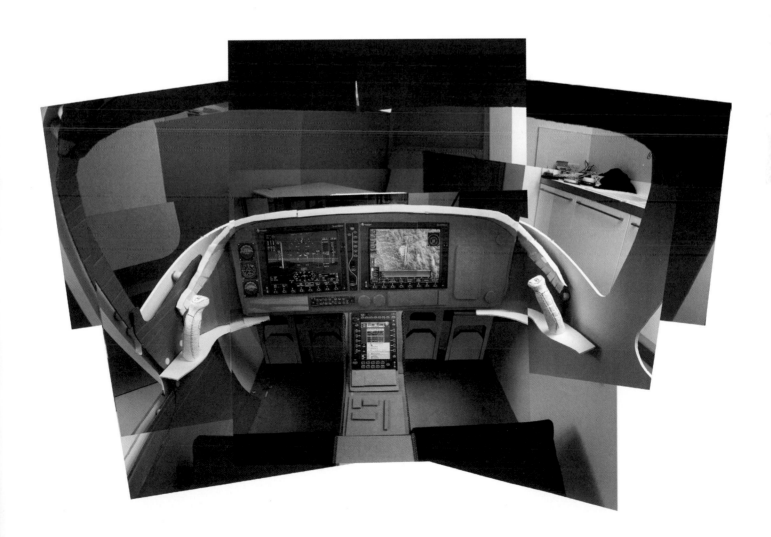

18

When Planet Corporate and
Planet Creative are aligned,
the shared vision means great
fortune may be in the stars.

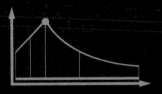

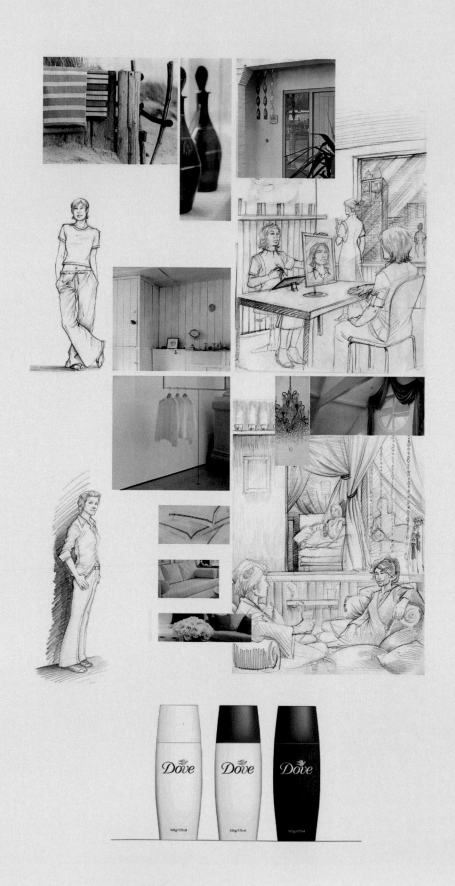

When corporates meet creatives

Unilever and Viadynamics | 2009

Search for images of 'a designer' on the Internet, and you are presented with a troubling quantity of pictures of men in big glasses wearing turtleneck jumpers. To the hard-nosed suits of big business, the creatures of the design world can appear like an alien species.

Ron Khan, then Packing Director at the Unilever-owned food giant Knorr, is honest about the strained relationship there can be between corporates and creatives. "Marketing would go to a design agency who would come up with some fancy idea, and our role in R&D and Supply Chain and Buying was to go 'Oh my God – what a ridiculous design! How can we get that to work?' Thankfully, I was given the chance to re-evaluate how we saw design," he says.

Khan was among a group of Unilever executives challenged to rethink everything they thought they knew about designers and design. A team from tangerine had a central role in a series of intensive four-day courses, initiated by Chris Thompson, founding partner of innovation consultancy Viadynamics.

"The Accelerating Innovation workshops were really about bringing design thinking into the corporate world," Thompson says. tangerine CEO Martin Darbyshire recalls: "You might have a branding person from London next to a chemist from Brazil or a technologist from India. They may be very good at what they do, but they have no complete picture of potential opportunities and their relevance to the consumer, brand and business."

The executives were divided up into teams, each with a tangerine designer to work with them. Over four short days, they were told, the teams would be taken on a 'design journey' from concept to prototype.

"The first two days were mighty confusing," Khan admits. "We were thinking about ideas like 'how do you disentangle design vision?'"

He was not alone in finding the first 48 hours of the project challenging. Video from one of the workshops identifies the word 'confused' as the overwhelming response to what they were being asked to do. "We took them on a hard and uncomfortable climb," Thompson accepts. His company's introduction to the course suggested participants "have to get properly lost" before they can find their way.

Left: Mood and story board from a workshop held to explore the potential of a spa concept for Dove.

"Then we bring them down again," says Thompson. "The process is like a ski-slope."

Khan vividly remembers the moment at the top of the mountain. "After two days the designers came in and started to sketch, and it was like BANG! WOW! This isn't just words we are chatting about. This is life."

Khan's team was working with Mike Woods. "My role was to get them to think like designers," Woods says. "We helped them visualise an outcome, helped them see that business plans cannot just rely on facts and figures."

The team had come up with the concept of 'food kits' – a way for people who don't have very advanced cooking skills to make healthy and delicious dishes. "It was an idea we thought could take Knorr away from stock cubes and into cooking aids," Khan says, "providing the components to make a meal."

Unilever executive Matthias Berger was also blown away by how the designers helped his team visualise their ideas. "Most people, including myself, are not visual thinkers," he says. "The ability to have an idea visualised cannot be underestimated."

Another team, led by tangerine partner Peter Phillips, was considering how to sell washing powder to African villagers. "It was amazing to see the change in thinking," Phillips recalls. "It chipped away at the mystique of 'the designer', the creatives being reluctantly brought in at the end of a project."

tangerine Creative Director, Matt Round, helped Unilever executives attempting to rethink frozen chocolate mousse. "We were trying to change the experience from getting a pot of mousse out and sticking your spoon into it. Could you share it in a different way? Maybe have a crust so you can pick it up. We christened it 'sushi mousse'!"

Below and right: Renders from the Knorr workshop exploring the potential of 'wet-sauce' with pre-prepared ingredients combined into a meal by the customer. All images and concepts were created during the three-day workshop with designers actively working with the client to explore and translate ideas.

"After two days the designers came in and started to sketch, and it was like BANG! WOW! This isn't just words we are chatting about. This is life."

Ron Khan, Packing Director, Knorr

Below: The Mountain & the Ski Slope, created by Viadynamics, is one of the fundamental tools that is used to design the innovation journey of a project.

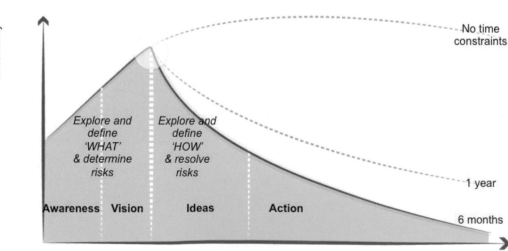

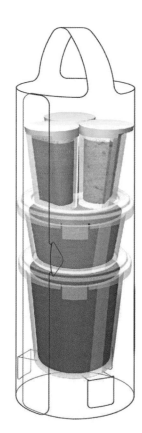

"The tangerine designers don't realise how much they know," says Thompson. "They have a fantastic ability to articulate ideas, visually and verbally. But they also understand the commercial reality of manufacturing and selling products."

At the end of the four days, each of the teams had a business case, a project charter and a 3D prototype. "It is probably the hardest I have ever worked," says Woods. "But it shows how much can be done in a very short space of time."

"We created something really phenomenal," says Khan. He took his idea for cooking kits back to Knorr, but colleagues didn't buy it. "It was too advanced," he sighs. "That was ten years ago, but now you see the same idea everywhere on the market."

Other prototypes from the Accelerating Innovation sessions did find their way into product development across the Unilever empire – new ideas for brands like Dove, OMO and Wall's ice-cream.

For Berger, it was the 'holistic' approach to design that was the real revelation. "Marketing-led design often creates something beautiful but not very practical. Technical design often creates something functional but not very beautiful. At the workshop, we were able to bring the two together."

It was also a chance to show just what is possible when you get alignment between Planet Corporate and Planet Creative.

Right: Concept sketch of the inital idea for frozen chocolate 'sushi-mousse'.

Left: Initial ideas are discussed and debated during the workshop and then drawn up by the designers. The concepts are developed with sketches and 3D CAD renders overnight, to show to the client the next day for final discusssion.

Left: A discussion of 'moments' when people could interact with an experience in a different way. In a dinner party environment (far left), a frozen chocolate mousse could be substituted for after dinner mints. A couple (left) share the same moment, but in a more intimate environment.

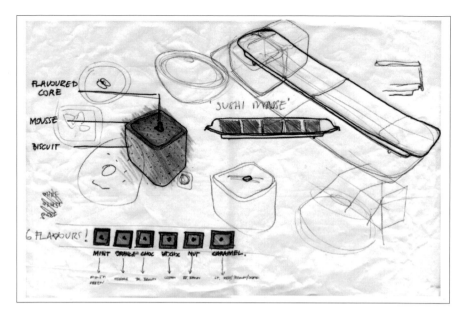

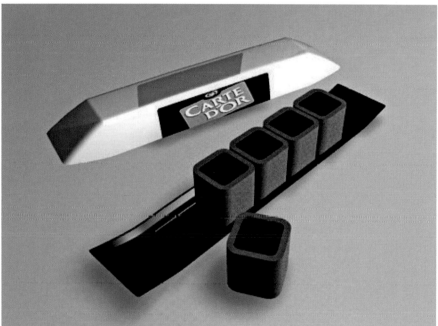

Above: 3D CAD concept modelled and rendered overnight of frozen chocolate mousse in a sushi form.

19

In defining business strategy
and brand direction, the
design process can sometimes
have a value greater than the
end product.

If the shoe fits

Dakota | 2010

As the economic giant that is modern Brazil strides into the global market, upon its feet are locally made shoes. The country has long had a reputation for having something of a foot felish – the feet of its soccer stars are worshipped, of course. But with annual production close to 900 million pairs of shoes a year, Brazil is now the third largest producer of footwear in the world.

For tangerine, eager to explore emerging economies, Brazilian footwear has helped them take steps into South America. "We are early in this market," says tangerine CEO Martin Darbyshire. "It is tough and fiercely competitive, but there are really interesting opportunities in Brazil. It's a great place to work and very design-sensitive."

In 2010, tangerine was encouraged by the remarkable economic expansion in Brazil to open an office in Porto Alegre, a city of 1.5 million people in the south of this vast country. Its first project was with the footwear manufacturer Dakota, a company producing 90,000 pairs of shoes every day.

"We were looking to develop for the first time a new casual shoe in our Kolosh range for the sports market and knew we needed a different approach for what is a very competitive market," says Marcelo Lehnen, CEO of Dakota. "We heard about tangerine from Pro Target, a Brazilian advertising agency, and they came with great references."

Dakota had previously concentrated on women's shoes, so a move into the male-dominated sportswear market was a significant shift. But Lehnen was after more than advice on shoe design – he wanted to know how design could help his firm expand. "European design agencies like tangerine have much more experience in how to enter major markets," Lehnen says. "We wanted to learn about the product development process and the complete focus on the customer."

Darbyshire packed his suitcase and headed for Nova Petrópolis, a German-speaking town in the foothills of Brazil's Gaucho Highlands, where Dakota has its headquarters. Travelling with him was Michael Thomson, from Design Connect, who has worked on projects with tangerine as a strategic brand consultant for more than a decade.

Left and below: Hand-drawing and sketching are still key tools when developing the form and features of dynamic products.

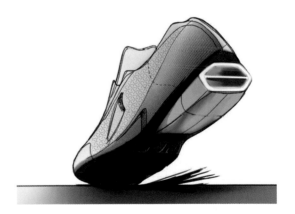

"Martin's been taking the company very quietly into a much broader understanding of what design can do for a client," Thomson says. "The consumer's experience of the product is critical to defining their perception of the brand and the brand is a bigger idea than the product itself. That is why it is necessary to understand where the business is going, what it's trying to achieve, what its underlying values are."

When they arrived, they organised a two-day workshop with executives from across Dakota's marketing, production and technology divisions. "It's about getting to a position of clarity as to what they are trying to do and why," explains Thomson. "By the time they have finished the two days, a lot of undergrowth will have been cleared!"

"At the end of the process," says Darbyshire, "we had helped them define a proposition for their brand strategy. Only then did we go on to work with them on a final design for a sports shoe."

The process was a revelation to the executives at Dakota. "It was the first kind of workshop like this we have ever done," says Lehnen. "The difference is the creative talent that they bring – they are very creative guys."

The visit was also a revelation for the two Brits. Despite the strong European influences, Brazil has developed its own distinct consumer culture, which needs to be understood. "Most people still pay for their shoes in instalments," Darbyshire notes. "It is mainly about needing to spread the cost, but for some women it is also apparently about hiding the true cost from their husbands!"

"The attention tangerine paid to the different cultural perspectives of the country was very important for us," says Lehnen. "We learned such a lot from the process even though the product concept itself has not reached the market."

A change in market circumstances may have meant tangerine's 'crazy heel' being dropped, but Dakota says they haven't given up on expanding their sports range. "Aspects of tangerine's design approach are being used in preparing other styles and products in our range," Lehnen says.

"There is an awakening to design in Brazil," says Darbyshire, who in 2013 was asked to address the first ever Design Week in Rio de Janeiro. For tangerine, Dakota and Kolosh will always be remembered as the footwear that walked them into an exciting new market.

Right: A two-day consultancy workshop organised for the Dakota team. Executives were helped to explore and define the company's mission vision and the brand proposition.

"We were looking to develop for the first time a new casual shoe in our Kolosh range for the sports market and knew we needed a different approach for what is a very competitive market."
Marcelo Lehnen, CEO, Dakota

Left: Brazilians recognise Kolosh shoes as a leisure brand for women. To increase potential sales, Dakota needed to expand the brand appeal to men and get the shoes sold in sports stores.

Right: The workshop defined a new clear brand framework – 'Viva Intensamente' (Live intensively).

Portugese

Vision

Nossa visao eh que a Kolosh seja reconhecida como uma das mais lembradas e amadas marcas de tenis esportivos do Brasil.

Mission

Estabelecer a Kolosh como tenis esportivo masculino no mercado brasileiro e simultaneamente aumentar o reconhecimento e participacao no segmento feminino, surpreendendo o mercado com nossos produtos inovadores garantindo o futuro da marca.

Values

**PAIXAO
ENERGETICO
DIFERENTE
FACIL RELACIONAMENTO
FORTE
CONFIANTE
IRREVERENCIA
ABERTO A NOVIDADES**

Proposition

VIVA INTENSAMENTE

LIVE INTENSIVELY

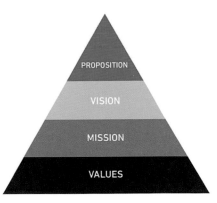

PROPOSITION

VISION

MISSION

VALUES

English

Vision

Our vision is for Kolosh to be one of the best known and loved Brazilian brands of sports leisure shoes from Brazil.

Mission

To establish Kolosh as a men's sports leisure shoe in the Brazilian market and simultaneously increase recognition and market share in the woman's segment, surprising the competitors with our innovative products to ensure the future of the brand.

Values

**ENERGETIC
DIFFERENT
OPEN
STRONG
CONFIDENT
IRREVERENT
FORWARD LOOKING**

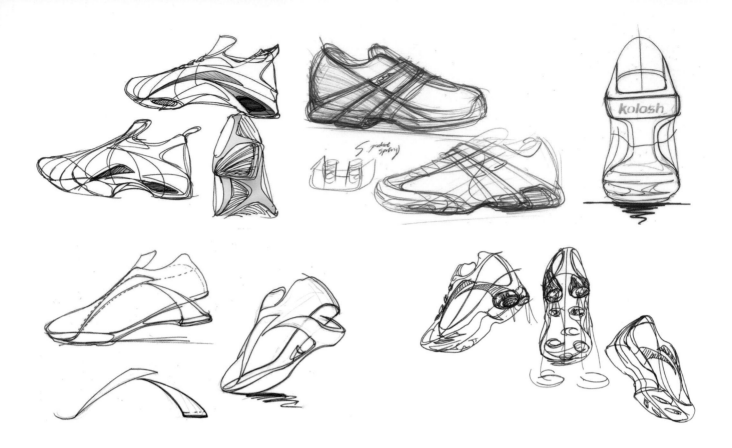

Above and right: Sketches showing the build of the concept. The form of the hollow heel is blended with the reformed Kolosh logo to integrate the brand and its product.

Below and left: More detailed sketches and final elevation renderings used to guide design and engineering of the production unit.

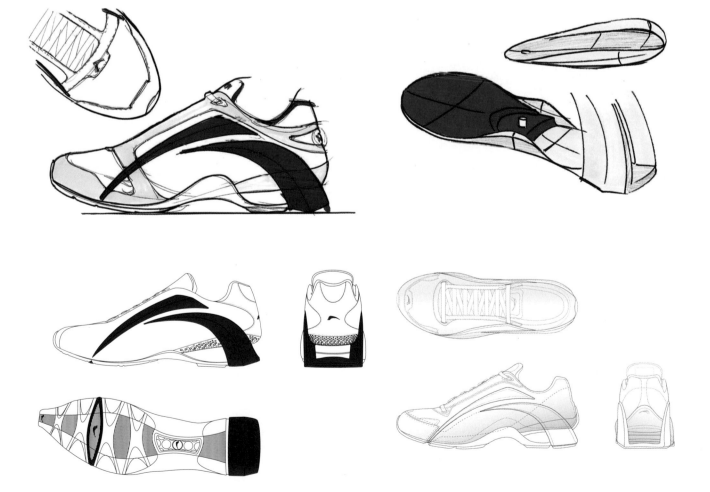

20

Thinking the unthinkable takes you on a journey to a destination that competitors wouldn't consider.

First Class experience

Heathrow Express | 2011

Think of the First Class compartment of an English railway train and one can almost smell the aroma of luxury mixed with fantasy and a hint of mystery. These days, travelling First Class is not quite cocktails on the Orient Express, but train operators know that attracting premium customers is critical to their business plan. For designers, the challenge is to create an ambience of elegance and style within the tight margins and constraints of a modern railway network.

When the first Heathrow Express slipped out of its platform at Paddington station in 1998, it carried with it a reputation for comfort, refinement and innovation. Fourteen years later and the trains were beginning to look their age. The company decided to commission a complete refit of both its standard and First Class carriages, looking to restore its name as a confident, high quality and premium service. The project was a four-way collaboration with rail consultancy Interfleet, engineering group Railcare and technology giant Siemens working alongside Heathrow Express (HEX). "The result," according to Heathrow Express Engineering Manager Mark Chestney, "was a design for standard carriages that looked fine, but First Class carriages that looked a bit clinical – no wow factor." The 'wow factor' is an essential ingredient in the premium travel market. The passenger experience, both emotional and functional, must set First Class apart from the standard offering. Customers must feel special.

As he pondered on how to make their First Class passengers feel properly valued, Chestney happened to attend a conference at which tangerine CEO Martin Darbyshire was explaining how his company had found the difference for BA's premium customers. "The penny dropped," says Chestney. "Martin stressed the importance of individuality and personal space – we just didn't have that in our First Class carriages." tangerine was invited to join the team.

Introducing a new player into the team halfway through the project was always going to present particular challenges. Siemens manager Gary Batchelor admits he was sceptical. "I questioned why we needed to bring in an external design contractor," he says. Describing himself as "an old railway hand", Batchelor says he "feared they would be all pink ties, fluffy slippers and ridiculous ideas".

Left: Vision for Heathrow Express First Class carriage, defining individual passenger space and privacy but with everything necessary to hand.

It wasn't easy for the team from tangerine either. Creative Director Matt Round applauded the courage of Heathrow Express in recognising they needed to be more ambitious, but was aware of the constraints in coming in when many of the key design decisions had already been taken. "Design can solve some problems, but not every one," he says, "and we know that if design is embedded from the start you have a greater chance of success."

The key on this project was to make a real difference to the passenger experience and, with that in mind, Round took a trip to Heathrow. "Sitting in First Class, I couldn't help but notice there were lots of seats with no one in them," he recalls. "So I thought – let's just get rid of them."

It was a truly radical idea – having just one passenger sitting on each side of the train corridor. No British commercial railway carriage had ever been configured this way. "I thought we should trade carriage capacity for customer privacy and exclusivity," Round says. The question was how the 'old railway hands' would react. "No other train operating company would consider it," Chestney confirms. "We quickly realised, though, that our occupancy was relatively low and that by reducing the number of seats you might actually boost it." Far better, he told colleagues, to have 100 seats that are 50 per cent full rather than 200 seats that are 10 per cent occupied.

It was a massive decision, opening up all kinds of new opportunities for the design team. "As old railway hands and engineers we tend to think in a certain way," Batchelor says. "tangerine directed us to think in another way."

The journey between Heathrow and central London can take as little as 15 minutes, a very limited time to impress the customer. The First Class experience had to begin from the moment the passenger stepped onto the station platform.

"We thought about every moment of the journey," Round says. "LED displays showing you which carriage to get on for which terminal, changing the entrance so people move through the cabin more easily, making the luggage storage more accessible and then displays inside the carriage changing colour to let you know when to get off. If you waste a minute on a short journey, it makes a difference."

It was also about the ambience, creating a modern aspirational space that exuded sophistication and elegance. For this, tangerine's experience of designing premium airline cabins for British Airways proved invaluable. "Our work on aircraft interiors helped a lot. We have developed a great deal of expertise and intuition about what premium passengers want," Round says. "The key is to deliver seclusion and privacy – having everything to hand, making it easy for passengers."

There were parts of the railway environment that provided liberation from the strictures of design in the skies for the tangerine team. "Trains have these wonderful picture windows and we were keen to use natural daylight to improve the journey experience," Round recalls. "We designed screening to use the light that comes in, so we could layer the overall lighting of the carriage, creating a more subtle feel."

The project meant monthly trips for Round to a mocked-up coach at the Railcare works in Wolverton near Milton Keynes. "The whole team was trying out various ideas," Chestney remembers. "Matt and his team would always come armed with books of different coloured carpet and laminate samples to get the look and feel just right."

Trains may offer design freedom unavailable on planes, but one tangerine idea with its origins in the sky proved impossible to implement.

"Design can solve some problems, but not every one. We know that if design is embedded from the start you have a greater chance of success."
Matt Round

"Occupancy levels have gone up significantly. Now people walk past First Class and think, 'I want to be in there.'"

Mark Chestney. Engineering Manager, Heathrow Express

"We couldn't do everything they wanted, " says Gary Batchelor. The proposal was that the First Class seats should be able to swivel so passengers could choose greater company or privacy. "It might work on an aircraft, but crash-worthiness regulations would have meant us taking 18 months just to seek approval," Batchelor explains. "Maybe someone will be brave in the future."

For tangerine, it was a project that called less for bravery and more for psychology – an understanding of how to deliver a First Class experience in just 15 minutes. The result delivered the 'wow factor' Heathrow Express had demanded.

"Occupancy levels have gone up significantly," says Chestney. "Now people walk past First Class and think, 'I want to be in there', whereas before they'd walk past and think, 'Why do I want to spend the extra money for that?'"

Right: Observational research of existing customers was key to unlocking insights.

Left: The Heathrow Express went into service in 1998 and was scheduled for overhaul.

Below left and right: Interior of previous Heathrow Express First Class carriage.

Below: Mapping of the customer journey was the starting point for redefining what the onboard experience could be.

Buy ticket on-line

Arrive at station

Buy ticket at station

Find platform and select train

Select carriage

Store luggage

Select seat

Con

Start	In transit	Departure Station

Right: Getting inside the customer's mind to understand what really matters to them on the short journey to and from Heathrow.

The first class passenger mindset...

Boarding with ease.
Being looked after.
Feeling relaxed and comfortable.
Not wanting to be disturbed.
Having their own private space.
Everything they need to hand.
Getting to their destination quickly with no fuss.

Below: Establishing hallmarks helped guide executives with an engineering background to understand and deliver a truly First Class travel experience.

Brand/service hallmarks

Privacy

Exclusivity

Service

Provenance

Detail

Departure time/destination

Show or buy a train ticket

Check exit for terminal

Check guide for all carriers at terminals

Collect luggage

Look for platform and exit

Leave train

Onboard

Arrive at destination

Smoked mirror glass to shield the carriage from the luggage

Glowing HEX logo. Hex Logo in carpet pattern

Duo-tone map of London Paddington & west end on bulkhead

Printed blinds on window to cast layered shadows across the carriages

LED information in the lobby

Layers of smoked glass

Deep tan leather seating

Left: The initial vision showing what elements could be changed, as presented to Heathrow Express.

Right: A re-designed carriage interior, redistributing space to provide each passenger with their own environment.

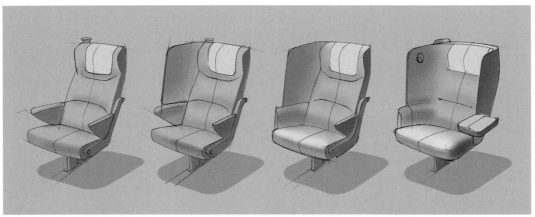

Left: Concept sketches showing a progressive level of change to the seating design.

Right: In addition to the design of the physical carriage, concepts for the digital services were developed for both on and off the train.

Existing

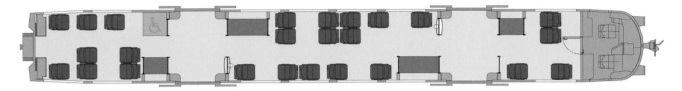

Revised

Above: Carriage entry vestibule featuring easy access and direction signage.

Above: New carriage
interior, showing the hat
racks removed, to reduce
costs, and the screen
printing on the windows to
create light and shadow.

Left: On-site work at the Railcare base in Wolverton, England.

Above and left: Interior carriage space with the radical single seat configuration.

21

Taking common threads from
a complex tapestry, and weaving
them into new and appealing
designs, is a route to outstanding
experiences.

Flying free from a tight spot

Asiana A380 | 2011

Great design is often about creating space in a tight spot. In the field of aircraft interiors this is true both literally and metaphorically. The physical parameters of the fuselage, stringent safety requirements and the confining complexity of a highly competitive global industry mean designers must call upon all their escapology skills.

When the South Korean airline Asiana ordered six of the world's largest passenger aircraft, the Airbus A380, they came to tangerine for advice on how to make the Business and First Class cabins look stunning. The British design company had a reputation for both brilliant work in the skies and a deep understanding of South Korea. "We chose tangerine because of their successful cabin interior design work, notably British Airways, and having an office located in Seoul meant we could expect the project to progress more quickly and efficiently," says Asiana's Design Manager Jongsuk Lee. "We needed a company with the know-how to manage the problems of different cultures and languages, as well as cope with the physical distance and time difference."

Key to getting the Asiana project off the ground was tangerine's President Don Tae Lee. "I spoke their language and understood their expectations," Don says. "My role was to communicate with Asiana

Left: Final design of Asiana's A380 First Class cabin.

Below: Mood boards exploring the new look and feel of the cabin.

and the tangerine team as to how we could really make the design process work."

But even with all their advantages, tangerine CEO Martin Darbyshire could see that this project was going to need all of his company's vast experience to pull off. "We were working on a First Class seat manufactured in Arizona, a Business Class seat made in France, a First Class galley and walls produced in Tokyo and with a bar and lounge area created in Germany," he says. "The client was based in Seoul and the aircraft were being assembled in Toulouse. We knew we had our work cut out."

The geographical complexity was only part of the challenge. When creating the ground-breaking flat-bed for BA, Darbyshire and tangerine had had the freedom to rethink the design from first principles. With this project, the Airbus interior layout and the seat structures were largely fixed before the project began. The challenge is to find the space within the confines of the cabin and the contract to remain creative. "It's about strategic thinking, exhaustive enquiry and attention to detail," says Darbyshire. "Although we didn't actually design any of the seat mechanism in this case, we were able to make subtle adjustments which freed us up to create significant improvements to the design."

One of the areas the Airbus manufacturers had left free for airlines to customise was the front of the upper deck. tangerine and Asiana executives had agreed this exclusive corner of the aircraft might be turned into a bar and lounge. "We thought that for customers to have a place they could go and sit away from their allocated seat in a quiet and calming space was an important differentiator," Darbyshire says. "The idea was that they could have a drink, sit on a sofa, relax and read a newspaper – we know this makes a big difference to people's well-being."

Even here, though, the bounds of aviation regulation meant compromise was necessary. "You are always trying to push airlines forward with new materials and innovation, but sometimes it has to be pulled back," says tangerine's CMF (colour, material and finish) expert Emma Partridge, who was responsible for the interior look of the cabins. "We wanted to install a striking, back-lit, onyx surface in the bar, but the complexity and risk of cracking meant we ended up choosing a laminate bar top lit from above with bronze paint finishes that give it gloss and shine."

Despite the concessions, clever use of colour and finishes meant the result was innovative and sophisticated. "It was a complex project with numerous aviation safety considerations," agrees Jongsuk Lee. "However, the partnership with tangerine gave us solutions to these challenges."

"The large First and Business Class bathrooms have mock timber flooring and a leather seat to sit on with a lovely white coral effect," Partridge says. "There is a big contrast between the fresh atmosphere in the bathroom and the warm and inviting feel of the lounge area."

Working on the interior design with Partridge was Junghyun Cho (Joey) from tangerine's Seoul office. Such were the geographical complexities of the contract that he ended up stationed in London to be closer to the assembly process in France when designing the Business Class seat. "We weren't able to modify the base engineering of the original seat structure, so the job was to make it look nicer," Joey recalls. "We changed all the surfaces, the shapes, even the height of the shell a little. At the end of a lot of travelling and a lot of meetings, Asiana were really happy with it."

Above: Exploration of CMF – colour, material and finish – of the interior.

"We were working on a First Class seat manufactured in Arizona, a Business Class seat made in France, a First Class galley and walls produced in Tokyo and with a bar and lounge area created in Germany. The client was based in Seoul and the aircraft were being assembled in Toulouse."
Martin Darbyshire

Right: Rendering of Business
Class seating.

Below: Photograph of
Asiana's A380 new Business
Class cabin.

Left and below: Overhead views of the A380 First Class cabin.

Above: A380 upper deck lounge and stairwell.

That sense of achievement is echoed by Patrice Boursiquot, Asia-Pacific General Manager of Sogerma, manufacturers of the Solstys business-class seat used in the A380. "It's one of the very best Solstys designs and the best co-operation we've had with the customer and the designer, " he says. "The line of communication with tangerine was excellent and the product is outstanding."

Darbyshire is delighted with the way his team navigated the airline contract through to a safe landing. "They are tricky projects because they involve a lot of work over a long period and with all the battles and challenges you must never lose sight of what matters – the quality of the end product," he says.

"Asiana likes calm and serene to be its style," says Don Tae Lee, who had finalised the exact design direction at every stage with Asiana's CEO. "Out of the intensity of this project, we maintained that sense of calm serenity while giving the airline a bit more direction and clarity."

The first of the giant A380s went into service in July 2014, carrying passengers between Seoul and Los Angeles, and Asiana are convinced they will contribute to what they envisage as the airline's "beautiful future and forward-looking spirit". "We believe we will have positive reviews," says Jongsuk Lee. "We expected many difficulties when we started, but our relationship with tangerine found the answers and we hope this positive partnership will continue."

"They are tricky projects because they involve a lot of work over a long period, and with all the battles and challenges you must never lose sight of what matters – the quality of the end product."
Martin Darbyshire

Above: Detailed images of First Class, clockwise – hanging space, seat back showing reading light, magazine storage and seat controller, and inflight entertainment controller.

Above: GUI (graphic user interface) of the seat controller.

22

Defining a vision for the future means knowing your starting point, identifying your goal and planning how you are going to cross the terrain.

Moving heaven and earth

Hyundai Heavy Industries | 2011

The city of Ulsan is the industrial powerhouse that has driven the remarkable expansion of South Korea. This coastal metropolis boasts the world's largest car plant and the world's largest shipyard. Above both shines one name – Hyundai. The word itself means 'modernity', and the company behind the vast shipbuilding works on the waterfront, Hyundai Heavy Industries (HHI), remains true to the pioneering spirit of founder Ju-yung Chung. The website talks of their determination "to reinvent ourselves through innovation".

"We were challenged by Hyundai Heavy Industries to see the future vision," says tangerine designer Junghyun Cho (known to all as Joey) "It was a new type of project for me, involving a huge amount of research." tangerine had been approached by Hyundai Heavy Industries with a daring proposal to design the future for their construction vehicles and to be as conceptual as they wanted. "This job was about showing just how forward-looking the Hyundai Heavy Industries brand was," tangerine President Don Tae Lee believes. "It was also about sending a message to Hyundai Heavy Industries' competitors."

For tangerine it was a rare opportunity to start with a blank sheet of paper and rethink the design of industrial workhorses – the forklift, the wheel-loader and the earthmover. "It was a great project for me," says Joey. "I did a huge number of initial sketches and came up with dozens of different design ideas for each vehicle."

The instigator of the concept vehicles project was Jae-Pil Choi, Product Design Manager of Hyundai Heavy Industries. "I really appreciated the effort tangerine put into their initial presentation – the research and the design strategy," he says. "Their biggest advantage, though, was having offices in Seoul because we have worked with overseas consultancies before and struggled with communication."

Good communication was going to be at a premium because, despite everyone wearing the regulation company uniform, different departments within Hyundai Heavy Industries had different visions for the project. "It was vital that we were available in Seoul," says Don Tae Lee. "In all we must have had 30 separate meetings with their in-house design team and their

Left: Concept design of interior of earth moving equipment.

Below: Internal workshop with tangerine and executives from Hyundai Heavy Industries in Ulsan, South Korea.

Bottom: Brand framework for Hyundai Heavy Industries, helping them to articulate their brand proposition.

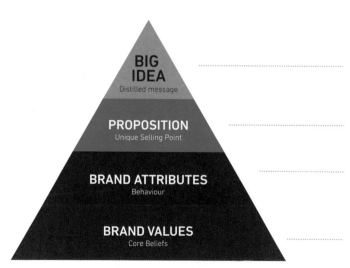

Big Idea
MOVING YOU FURTHER

Proposition
A business that sees beyond and goes further, pioneering with new product and service innovations that surprise competitors and delight customers

Brand Attributes
RESPONSIVE
CONNECTED
CAPABLE

Brand Values
TRUST
RELIABILITY
ORDER

BIG IDEA
Distilled message

PROPOSITION
Unique Selling Point

BRAND ATTRIBUTES
Behaviour

BRAND VALUES
Core Beliefs

HEAVY INDUSTRIES CO.,LTD.

"This job was about showing just how forward looking the Hyundai Heavy Industries brand was, it was also about sending a message to their competitor."

Don Tae Lee

engineering department discussing every aspect of the technology." Jae-Pil admits that it was a difficult and complicated process. "The business department wanted simply to update the existing models while the design department and tangerine wanted something much more innovative and conceptual. In the end I made the decision to go with concept vehicles."

From Joey's pile of sketches emerged designs for three extraordinary futuristic vehicles – concepts that trade journalists suggested would have looked quite at home in some space-age science-fiction movie.

"I am proudest of the excavator because it will bring a lot of benefits to the driver," Joey says. "We created extendable caterpillars to change the centre of gravity, allowing the machine to operate on the most irregular terrain while the cabin always remains horizontal." The compact forklift also had an ingenious feature. "I solved the big problem that forklift drivers cannot see in front when large boxes have been loaded," Joey claims. "We loved the way the cab could spin completely around," agrees Jae-Pil. "We have never seen that on any other vehicle." The earthmover had a creative solution to an old problem, too. "When stuff is lifted you often get water and small particles in the bucket that you don't want," Jae-Pil explains. "tangerine incorporated clever little holes so that waste material could be lost with the water."

The designs blew people away. "The concept models were so successful that Hyundai Heavy Industries asked us to make a second set so they could take them to different countries around the world," Don said. "Lots of people loved the futuristic machines," agreed Joey.

Hyundai Heavy Industries installed them in the entrance hall of their European headquarters and after appearing at the Conex design show in Seoul, the company decided to exhibit them at events in the United States, Germany and France.

"Our engineers were amazed," Jae-Pil confirms, "especially the overseas sales division." The vehicles' journey from concept to reality has not yet been completed, but the company has said it may only be five years or so before some of the ideas can be applied to working machines.

"These concept models provide a symbol of our ambition and a message to our customers," says Jae-Pil. The designs were a statement of intent from Hyundai Heavy Industries and a reflection of tangerine's creativity, true to the pioneering principles of both companies.

"These concept models provide a symbol of our ambition and a message to our customers."

Jae-Pil Choi, Product Design Manger, Hyundai Heavy Industries

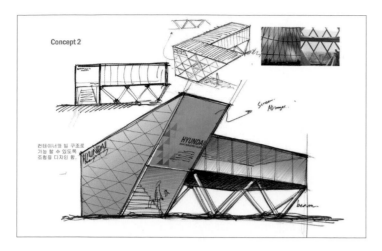

Concept 2

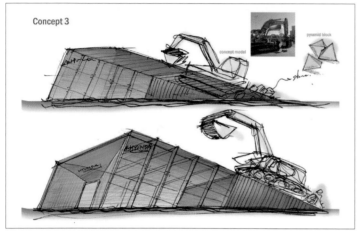

Concept 3

Above: Research and analysis of products around the world.

Below: Insight research and user observation of current products.

– 슬리퍼로 바꿔 신고 작업
– 캐빈공간이 좁아 수납공간도 협소
– 별도로 네비게이션 장착

– 신발을 별도의 통에 넣어서 보관
– 다양한 공구들이 널려 있음
– 에어컨을 켠채 문을 열고 작업함

– 상체 아래 공간이 지저분함

– 구리스통을 항상 싣고 다녀야 함

– 캐빈 공간이 넓어져 운전자가 작업 후 쉬는 동안 좌석을 뒤로 젖히고 쉴 수 있음

– 대부분의 사용자들은 브랜드 (Robex)에 대해 잘 알지못한다.

– 대부분의 사용자들이 시야 확보를 위해 별도의 버스용 후방미러를 장착한다고 함

– 신차 구입 시 추가 옵션에 대한 비용 부담이 커 대부분 소규모 공업소 등에서 구입 및 장착함

Left: Initial ideas and
opportunities to improve
usability and user
experience.

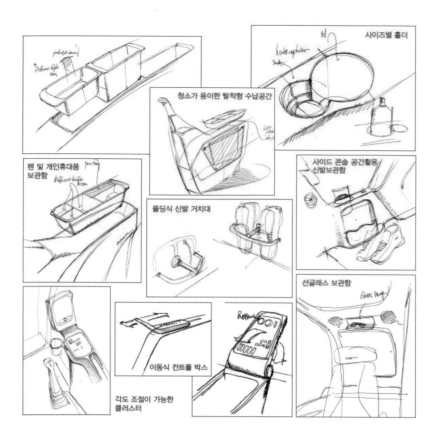

사이즈별 홀더

청소가 용이한 탈착형 수납공간

펜 및 개인휴대품 보관함

사이드 콘솔 공간활용 신발보관함

폴딩식 신발 거치대

선글라스 보관함

이동식 컨트롤 박스

각도 조절이 가능한 클러스터

Right: Developed ideas of
new interior.

"The business department wanted simply to update the existing models while the design department and tangerine wanted something much more innovative and conceptual. In the end I made the decision to go with concept vehicles."
Jae-Pil Choi, Product Design Manger, Hyundai Heavy Industries

Sketches showing how the design language could be implemented on current products from Hyundai Heavy Industries.

A future vision for the Hyundai Heavy Industries Excavator.

"Our engineers were amazed, especially the overseas sales division."

Jae-Pil Choi, Product Design Manger, Hyundai Heavy Industries

Right: Fork Lift.

Below: Earth Mover.

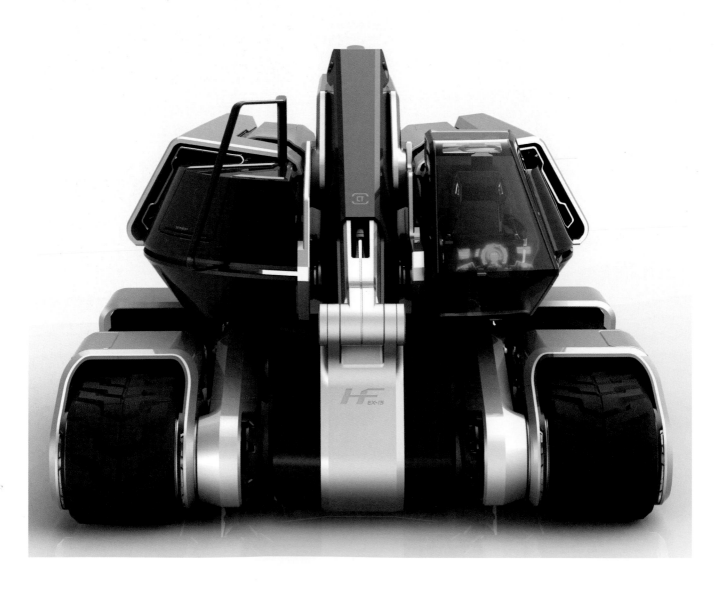

23

Turning a business into a
brand is like turning players
into a team: the strategy needs
to be in place before flair and
skill can play their part.

Rising stars of the big screen

BOE | 2013

BOE is a young company in a hurry. Wang Dongsheng, Chairman of the 20-year-old Chinese technology giant, tells his staff that "quality and speed are the keys of victory" as the firm looks to take advantage of the rapid expansion of the global high-definition television market.

The name may not yet mean much to those outside the field of digital displays, but BOE is already one of the world's biggest manufacturers of LCD video panels, supplying Samsung, LG and other multinationals. "Now, instead of just supplying others," says tangerine CEO Martin Darbyshire, "they want to create their brand and develop their own name in China."

The British designers were invited to help BOE develop two top-of-the-range 4K 140cm (55in) HD televisions for the burgeoning home market. "We knew what we had so far didn't have the DNA of BOE," says Wang Ying, Assistant Manager at the company. "So, we invited tangerine to help us to finish the project."

Even before Darbyshire and tangerine's Chinese-born Project Manager and Senior Designer Weiwei He made their first presentation at BOE's corporate HQ in Beijing, the clock was ticking. "They had a very 'efficient' schedule," Darbyshire jokes. "We started the project in March 2013, worked intensively with the BOE engineers until June, and a year later the TVs were on sale."

Efficiency, perhaps, is in the blood of this state-run enterprise that began making equipment for the Chinese military. "The first thing we all agreed on was that, in this market, size matters," Darbyshire remembers. "Right now, lots of people are buying new apartments in China and a giant TV is a must-have product. What we didn't have a clear view of was how BOE wanted to be distinctive in such a crowded market."

Discussion centred on what was meant by 'premium' product, what additional 'value' BOE might offer and how the role of television in the home might change in the future. "These were the questions we needed to ask," Darbyshire says. "All televisions seem the same," Weiwei agrees. "The challenge was how to stand out and be different." Consumers wanted big screens, but market research demonstrated that image and sound quality were the most important aspects. "The panels offered brilliant picture

We believe that BOE could be...

"EXPERTS in cutting-edge manufacture"

"MASTERS in the world of home entertainment"

"CREATORS of visual statement pieces"

Above: Presentation to senior management team at BOE's Beijing headquarters, examining what space the company could own in the global television market.

Left: 3D rendering of the 4K 140cm (55in) LED HD TV with sound bar.

quality, so our advice was to integrate an additional speaker with enhanced sound quality into a simple and elegant design," says Weiwei.

The BOE management were delighted with the idea. "The product was refreshing," Wang Ying says. "We are hopeful that it will establish BOE as a high-end producer in the Chinese market."

Previous work that tangerine had done with the electronics giant LG meant that they already had a detailed understanding of how the television market was likely to develop. "TV won't become a computer because it will remain a 'lean back' rather than a 'lean forward' activity," Darbyshire explains. "The issue is differentiation because, as televisions become thinner and thinner, there's a lot less to give an identity to."

Working across continents, tangerine's designers and BOE's engineers attempted to deliver on that challenge. "We had a conference call almost every day during the design stage," Wang Ying recalls. "It was a pleasant experience. We used a popular instant messaging tool, WeChat, that can deliver voice and images instantly."

The tangerine team introduced BOE to a three-step approach: understanding the consumer market; devising a concept reflecting consumer trends; and manufacturing the product. "Chinese companies are very practical – they want to use design to generate business rather than being an end in itself," says Weiwei. "We educated them on how to use design as a business tool."

From the process of helping BOE design a premium television, tangerine shaped a brand identity for the company as a whole. "We can bring something different from a typical design consultancy," argues Darbyshire. "We look to make something distinctive for a company like BOE, aggressively trying to grow its brand."

Wang Ying confirms that BOE intends to build upon the style and quality of the HD television products. "I was in London for that project and saw tangerine's devotion to the work and the focus on the customer," she says. "We hope that we can establish a long and co-operative relationship with tangerine."

"... instead of just supplying others, they want to create their brand and develop their own name in China."
Martin Darbyshire

Above right: Stimulus boards with premium product imagery to help identify distinct characteristics of alternative design directions.

Right: Hand-drawn sketches displaying a multitude of design ideas used here for executive group work, exploring what BOE can own in the market. Line drawing is a still a crucial design skill and often overlooked.

Is it about VOIDS or NEGATIVE SPACES?

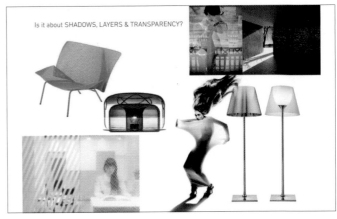

Is it about SHADOWS, LAYERS & TRANSPARENCY?

Is it about ILLUSION or a SENSE OF MAGIC?

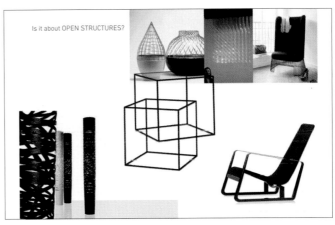

Is it about OPEN STRUCTURES?

Left: Various stages of model making.

Below: Final rendering of one of the first home entertainment systems, with the media hub integrated into the stand.

"Quality and speed are the keys of victory."
Wang Dongsheng, Chairman, BOE

Left and below: The remote control provides a great opportunity to improve the user experience. Simplifying the controls and establishing a closer relationship between the remote and on-screen user interface delivers real benefit.

24

Identifying a successful corporate strategy is like catching an individual snowflake in a blizzard: one must be exposed to the elements, open to opportunity and immersed in ideas.

Finding the power source of creativity

Nikon | 2013

Synonymous with precision optics for almost a century, Nikon is a global brand with a reputation for quality cameras and lenses, promising cutting-edge technology and clear vision. It is a market, though, being transformed before everyone's eyes – change so dramatic and rapid it is a struggle to maintain focus on what is going on. New gadgets and new ways of using them are popping up everywhere.

Nikon know this is a critical time for their industry and their business. Trying to determine the future of photography and particularly the user interface from the boardroom in Tokyo, though, was not an option. "There are many different ways of seeing the world, cultural differences that are very hard to understand sitting in Japan," says Nikon Group Manager Nobuya Kawahata. "With Nikon aiming to expand its global business, we decided to send one member of our team on a mission to discover and bring back the latest ideas and ways of thinking."

So it was that one of Nikon's rising star designers, Hiroki Hosaka, arrived at the offices of tangerine in London. "It was my first visit to Europe and everything was new and fresh for me," Hosaka recalls. "In Japan, typical corporate workers spend most of their time in meetings or dealing with paperwork. With the tangerine designers, most of their energy and time was spent on simply being creative!"

Nikon had approached tangerine because they had a reputation for extraordinary creativity in one of the most creative cities in the world. But there was something else about the London-based experience that was to be critically important in shaping Hosaka's ideas for how Nikon should target the global market. "The thing that left the greatest impression upon me, if I can put it in a single word, was 'diversity'," Hosaka says. "We did a workshop with around 16 students and there must have been ten different nationalities in the group!"

"We chose London because it is a cutting-edge 'design city' but also because it has a great history and a variety of cultures," Kawahata confirms. "Among the senior staff at tangerine, for example, was a Japanese designer who could provide vital support in communication and cultural bridging."

tangerine's Project and Creative Lead Yuichi Ishihara and Creative Director Matt Round took Hosaka under their wing. "There wasn't really a brief for the project at the beginning," Round recalls. "It was exploratory,

Left: A wall of ideas explored through imagery and discussion.

nothing explicit, just a very open brief to think about the future of the global camera market and develop Hiroki's professional capabilities as part of our design immersion programme."

"The most valuable thing for Nikon was this guy's education," says Ishihara. "They were targeting Hiroki as a future leader and so we were being asked to expose him to new ways and processes, visions and ideas."

First, tangerine immersed the young Japanese designer in the amazing cultural mix of 21st-century London. They literally wandered around the UK capital, soaking up the diversity and vitality of the city. A series of workshops had given Hosaka the 'trained insight' to translate what he saw into potential business opportunities. "It was an incredible experience and gave me a great opportunity to step back and reconsider my ideas about design, creativity and my whole way of thinking," Hosaka says. "London, with all its different nationalities, was a power source of creativity."

The tangerine team also took him on a whistle-stop European tour they described as a 'culture hunt'. "Nikon wanted him to get his head round the way that people in every country around the world are different, so we took him to six countries in two weeks," says Ishihara.

To an outsider, Hosaka might have been mistaken for the classic Japanese vacationer, armed with a Nikon and snapping away at every tourist attraction he encountered. In fact, he was building up a library of ideas that his bosses hope might inform the Japanese camera business for years to come.

"The smart phone is a key threat to the camera market," Round says. "That became entirely obvious to Hiroki when we ran a workshop with students at Central Saint Martins. He was absolutely flabbergasted that none of the students owned a camera and didn't really want one either."

Hosaka noticed how Europeans experimented with the cameras on their phones, finding new uses and starting new trends almost by accident. From watching and listening to students and young people from a wide range of cultural backgrounds, he began to realise that a purely technology-based business strategy missed the point. "Thanks to the project with tangerine, I began to look at things and think about ideas in a completely different way," Hosaka explains. "Now I want to share that thinking and attitude with my colleagues so we can really take advantage of that insight."

The culmination of the project was a presentation at Nikon headquarters in Tokyo. Hosaka, flanked by the team from tangerine, attempted to bridge the cultural divide and communicate the insight he had absorbed.

"He told them how photography has changed, the different social trends that have developed," Ishihara remembers. "He explained how, within European culture, cameras are about sharing rather than something personal and private. Photography is now a communication tool."

Hosaka also outlined a range of innovative ideas tangerine had developed for cameras of the future. "I got an incredibly positive response from the chief executive," Hosaka says. "He said it was 'absolutely fascinating', and I am sure my experience in London will have an enormous impact and inspiration on the future products and success of the Nikon Corporation."

"This piece of work and pieces like it, are about spreading the culture of design throughout an organisation from Chief Executive to junior team members. If you get the culture right, everything else follows," says Matt Round." The future of design, of great consumer experiences and successful organisations, rests on the quality and culture of the environments that businesses create for it to operate in."

"Thanks to the project with tangerine, I began to look at things and think about ideas in a completely different way. Now I want to share that thinking and attitude with my colleagues so we can really take advantage of that insight."
Hiroki Hosaka, User Interface Designer, Nikon

Right: Insight research and mapping, predicting the strongest opportunities and informing design exploration.

Below left: One of many team discussions.

Below right: Insight workshop with design students.

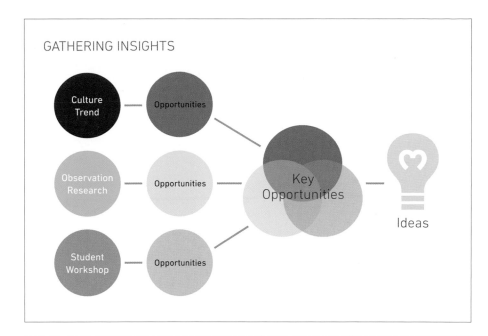

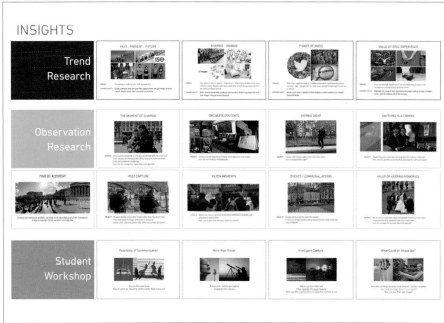

Europe through the lens of a
Japanese camera – Nikon
and tangerine designers on a
European cultural safari.

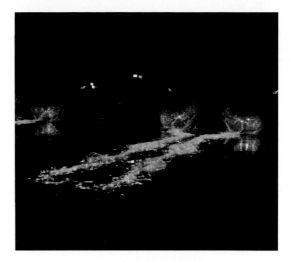

"This piece of work and pieces like
it, are about spreading the culture of
design throughout an organisation
from Chief Executive to junior
team members. If you get the culture
right, everything else follows, The
future of design, of great consumer
experiences and successful
organisations, rests on the quality
and culture of the environments
that businesses create for design to
operate in."
Matt Round

25

Design can deliver big messages
in small spaces. Sometimes
traditional techniques are the
best currency.

Above: The minted 50p coin designed to commemorate the 2014 Commonwealth Games in Glasgow, Scotland.

Great honour in small change

Royal Mint | 2013

When an invitation from the Royal Mint arrived, the designers at tangerine knew they were being challenged to step outside their comfort zone. The letter asked them to submit designs for 50-pence pieces celebrating the Glasgow 2014 Commonwealth Games. If they were successful, pieces of original tangerine design would reside in millions of pockets and purses for decades to come. This competition, should they win it, was less about profit and more about prestige.

Designing coins of the realm has traditionally been the province of artists and sculptors. Those granted the honour of having their bas-relief designs approved for public currency include David Gentleman and Sir Anthony Caro.

At tangerine, Senior Designer Dan Flashman assembled a team to consider the brief from the Royal Mint. "As we are a multi-cultural office, we gathered people from all over the world – which felt right, as this is a Commonwealth Games coin," Flashman explains. "We wanted lots of people to have an input."

The submission invitation initially asked for a design for the reverse of four 50-pence coins "which will capture the significance and friendly spirit of the Commonwealth Games". The Royal Mint Advisory Committee would inspect the entries and choose a winner, with final approval from the Chancellor of the Exchequer and, ultimately, the Queen herself. "To represent the vastness of the Commonwealth Games on a single 50 pence is difficult," Flashman admits. "We decided the coins must feature national elements like the flags, and the lettering needed to reflect the heritage of the particular country."

Among the team was Alex Loudon, fresh out of design school and relishing the challenge represented by the unusual 'equilateral curve heptagon' canvas of the 50-pence piece. "It was totally new for all of us," he says, recalling how they manipulated thistles and athletes, flags and text into hundreds of different positions. "You end up staring at it for hours."

From more than 50 different designs, the tangerine team selected their submission to the Advisory Committee meeting in the grand surroundings of the Worshipful Company of Cutlers' Hall in the City of London. Kevin

Right: First concepts submitted to the Royal Mint Advisory Committee.

Far right: Developed final sketches approved by the Royal Mint, Glasgow 2014, the Chancellor of the Exchequer and finally by Royal Proclamation.

"As we are a multi-cultural office, we gathered people from all over the world – which felt right, as this is a Commonwealth Games coin. We wanted lots of people to have an input."
Dan Flashman

Clancy, Committee Secretary and Director of the Royal Mint Museum, says, "What the Committee loved was the tone of what tangerine did – the spirit, the imagination and the intelligence." After short-listing tangerine's four designs, however, the Royal Mint decided to simplify the brief to just one coin. "The Committee wanted something very, very Scottish – Saltire and all," says Clancy.

For the tangerine team it was back to the drawing board and the tracing paper, searching for a design that would contain the essence of Glasgow, Scotland and the wider Commonwealth – all within the 27.3mm (1.075in) diameter of a 50-pence coin.

"We narrowed the designs down, choosing a runner and a cyclist as two sports to showcase," Loudon explains. "Sir Chris Hoy and the velodrome were very much on our minds!" The runner, originally a man, became a female sprinter and tangerine were given advice by Glasgow 2014 to ensure the angle of the athlete's legs reflected authentic sprinting technique.

The text also threw up challenges. The team used their own take on Scottish designer Charles Rennie Mackintosh's Classic font, but a layout which split the word 'Commonwealth' was rejected by the Advisory Committee. "We had to make sure Glasgow 2014 as a brand was being represented properly," says Clancy. "At each stage the tangerine team was well disciplined and responded to specifics."

It was always a team project, but the final winning submission was credited to young designer Alex Loudon. "We thought we had strong elements that summed up the athletic spirit of the Games," he says. "We used the Scottish Saltire in a very subtle way, but the final design was one people could recognise and understand."

The Advisory Committee agreed and the Royal Mint's engraving team were brought in to advise on the technical details. "Some parts needed more definition, and we needed to work out which parts would be raised and polished and which indented," says Flashman.

The Chancellor and the Queen clearly had no objections. The Royal Proclamation was issued and, with a master die expertly produced, Dan and Alex were able to witness the coin coming off the Mint presses in Wales at more than 800 a minute.

"Imagine going down to your local shop and actually getting something you designed in your change," says Alex. "It is very exciting and very strange."

And he even has his initials on it. The embedded 'AL' is tiny – but the only other person to enjoy the honour of being represented on a coin, apart from the designer, is the Queen.

"What the Committee loved was the tone of what tangerine did – the spirit, the imagination and the intelligence."
Dr Kevin Clancy, Secretary to the Royal Mint Advisory Committee on the Design of Coins and Director of the Royal Mint Museum

Index

Credits

Mel Yates: 8, 10, 13, 40, 44, 50
Moggy Photographer: 8, 16, 19, 30, 31, 40,
45, 54, 56, 57 (bottom left), 60
John Munro: 11, 13
Beth Austen: 35 (top right)
David Burton: 48
Dario Rumbo: 65
Mouse in the House: 86 (bottom left)
Woodmouse: 88
Andy Cameron: 92, 97, 98, 99
Jodi Hinds: 254 (top)

All other pictures supplied by clients.

Every effort has been made to
acknowledge correctly and contact the
source and/or copyright holder of each
picture and Carlton Books Limited
apologises for any unintentional errors or
omissions, which will be corrected in
future editions of this book.

tangerine London 2014

Ruth Barrett
Young Eun Choo
Martin Darbyshire
Melinda Darbyshire
Daniel Flashman
Gavin Flowers
Joy Grover
Weiwei He
Yuichi Ishihara
Don Tae Lee
Alex Loudon
Vien McArthur Nguyen
Martin Mo
Emma Partridge
Liza Fredrikke Rosenkilde Christensen
Matt Round
Monica Sogn
Lucas Tretout

tangerine Seoul 2014

Younglong Lee
Younwoo Chang
Junghyun Cho
Jeesu Hwang
Youngkyu Kim
Jinyoung Kim
Youngjae Kweon
Dontae Lee
Juhoon Lee
Jongrok Lee
Jihyun Lim
Kyungeun Seong
Seoyoung Shin
Jiyeon Yoon
Junho Yoon

tangerine Porto Alegre 2014

Annie Müller
Alexandre Lise

Above: Mike Woods

Below: Looking forward,
tangerine Porto Alegre 2014

Acknowledgements

There are many people who have helped us pull-together 25 years of memories and business know-how. Our first huge thank you goes to Antonia Higgs who stopped us from becoming design nerds and who makes the words fly off the page. Datuk' Professor Jimmy YK Choo OBE we are grateful for your support and kind words. Next is Carlton Publishing: Clare Baggaley, Katie Baxendale, Vanessa Daubney, Peter Dawson and Gemma Maclagan Ram, for whom patience is a virtue, and Jonathan Goodman for believing in us. Thank you Tim Potter for feedback, brainstorming and just being here. To all the wonderful people who gave freely of their time, many of whom are quoted within the pages, we thank you. Iobe Aleksander, Bob Ayling, David Baird, Jonathan Barratt, Gary Batchelor, Dame Anne Begg MP, Matthias Berger, Patrice Boursiquot, Robert Brunner, Jamie Cassidy, Mark Chestney, Jae-Pil Choi, Ju-yung Chung, Kevin Clancy, Mirjam van Coillie, Wang Dongsheng, Brian Drumm, Peter Cooke, Jon Florsheim, Paul Frankish, Tim Frost, Martin George, Paul Gregory, Chris Hill, Jongsuk Lee, Professor Kun-Pyo Lee, Tae-Kyung Lee, Marcelo Lehnen, Manfred Hubert, Malcolm Johnston, Ron Khan, Paul Kirtley, Seung Min Kim, Youngho Kim, Nobuya Kawahata, Hiroki Hosaka, Simon May, Emma Partridge, Sara Piteira, Will Pocknell , Dr Woo Suk-Hyung, Taek-Jong Shin, Ray Sterling, Chris Thompson, Michael Thomson , Andrew Wallace, Bin Xie, Wang Ying, Thom Verheggen, Professor Dr. Peter Zec, without you our story would lack impact. To the many tangerine alumni, without whom there would be no projects to talk about, we thank you, in particular: Clive Grinyer, Jonathan Ive, Heather Martin, Peter Phillips, David Tonge and Mike Woods.